SIGNS OF GRACE

GEORGE GOYDER

SIGNS OF GRACE

WITH ADDITIONAL CHAPTERS

BY ROSEMARY GOYDER

THE CYGNET PRESS
LONDON

Published by The Cygnet Press
46 Lexington Street, London W1

Typesetting by Alan Gray
Printed and bound by Smith Settle

Contents

CHAPTER I

Birth & Rebirth

I was born on the 22 June 1908. At the end of 1919 when I was twelve my parents brought my two brothers and myself back from the U.S.A. after six years abroad. I had been to kindergarten in Webster Groves, a suburb of St Louis, Missouri, and then to elementary school in New Rochelle, New York. School places were hard to find in Britain immediately after the first world war, and my parents had little choice, with the result that my elder brother Cecil and I were sent to Margate College, Kent. It was not a happy school, and bullying was not confined to the boys. One master (Mr G) had a habit of calling a boy out in front of the class for some misdemeanour and knocking him down with a sudden blow to the head. Another of Mr G's tricks was to call 'all eyes ahead' and come behind a boy unawares and give him a violent shove with his knuckles in the back of the neck so as to bang the head on the desk.

With my U.S.A. accent and my American knickerbockers, I was fair game... 'Yank, so you won the War!' was a common greeting, accompanied by a blow.

It was not my parents' fault. Father had to return to the U.S.A. on business, leaving my mother in her native Switzerland with my young brother Claude, while Cecil soon moved from Margate to Mill Hill School where he was found a place as a day boy, thanks to my parents' friendship with the headmaster, Sir John McClure. With my father travelling in U.S.A. and mother being in Switzerland, I had to stay at school during the Easter (1920) holiday. I was not happy, but at this time we had no home. On Good Friday I wrote my mother in Switzerland:

'Today all the boys went home. I got a platform ticket and saw the boys off. It was a happy time for everyone... today which is Good Friday it is raining again and so we must shudder in the cold under the worst master (Mr G) in the College. It is awfully miserable here in bad weather… my feet are nearly freezing and there is no warmth. What we must all wish for is good weather. So far, so good, and I am perfectly happy.'(!)

All this was bearable and scarcely a matter for complaint, or even for comment. My clothes were an altogether different matter. Clothes represented one's passport to respectability and it was wise to conform, if only to buy peace. The following is a postscript to the concluding part of a letter of thanks for birthday gifts.

1 July 1920

'P.S. dear dad,
I have a few matters of importance which I wish to tell you. The first and by far the most important is about my clothes. During the last holidays you told me not to worry until you get back. But now the time has come when I must tell you about my clothes. Ever since the beginning of this term I have been having a hard time because of my awful clothes. My *best* suit has three patches on the seat of the trousers, four in the front, three in the sleeves and in numerous other parts. My friends refuse to have anything to do with me on Sundays because of my clothes and everyone makes awful remarks. There is only one word which can tell what I really am on Sundays, an *Outcast*. *The boys in Margate College actually know that I wear Cecil's everyday trousers on Sunday*!!! Major Allen (master) always looks at me with disgust.

Now about my everyday suit. The trousers are patched front, back and on both legs, but they are better than my best suit… there is just one more thing. I have not been able to have any sports, cricket, etc. yet this term because I have no flannels and white shirt. When I have to play in the Junior 1st XI of our cricket club I promise the boy my pocket money for a half-week and borrow his trousers. This is the only way… Mr Leach Lewis (head master) will get the suit for you if you wish. I don't know what will happen if I don't have one by next Sunday. I hope that I am not worrying you by telling you all these things, but I hope that you see what an awful fix I am in, in not having any clothes to wear.'

I do not remember the result of this special pleading but it appears to have had the right effect. My father may have been deliberately hardening me off, but he never admitted anything!

At Whitsun (1920) I had the most important experience of my life: a determining event. It was Whit Sunday evening and Canon Pryor, Vicar of Margate, was preaching. He spoke about the power of prayer. 'It can do anything,' he said. 'It is the greatest power on earth.' Being miserable, I listened (for once) and while Canon Pryor was speaking I came to a determination. I would take the Canon at his word and pray with all my might, even if it were to crack the heavens open!

That night, after lights were out and the nine or ten boys in my dormitory asleep, I crept out of bed and prayed. Prayed with all my might and main, until I thought the Heavens would indeed crack. But nothing happened, although I felt better and went straight to sleep. Then the miracle occurred. I woke up to find myself completely surrounded by light of inconceivable brightness while a thrilling voice spoke to me words of total re-assurance. 'All shall be well, I am with you always.' It was indeed a miracle, and the turning point in my life. I was changed, re-born and reassured.

In the School Sports next day I won three prizes, never having won anything before. I had a new confidence. (I must admit when the boy I most feared next punched me, I punched him back; and that ended the bullying.)

A strange thing had happened to me about six months earlier. Before returning to school after the Christmas holidays, when the family were for a time together at my grandmother's house in Turnham Green, I was introduced to a business colleague of my father's named Barker. We shook hands on my way to bed. Mr Barker made no impression, good or bad. He seemed a little large and self-important and that was all. Next day I was back at school. After several days I found myself thinking constantly about Mr Barker and became more and more uneasy. Mr Barker was interfering with my sleep. Night after night I couldn't sleep, I became alarmed. I must do something. But what?

Every Monday we wrote a formal letter to our parents under the eye of the master. When I took my letter back to my desk after it had been read and approved, I remained standing for a moment at my desk with my back to the master and in that position tore a strip of blotting paper off the pad on my desk and wrote ten words before stuffing it in and sealing the letter. The ten words were: 'Don't trust Mr Barker. I can't sleep because of him.'

When my mother got my letter, she was worried and puzzled. Father was by now in New York. There were no transatlantic telephones then and letters took several days. So she telegraphed my exact words. My father immediately cabled the bank to stop withdrawals from his joint account with Mr Barker. But Mr Barker had already got away with several thousand pounds and my father lost a substantial sum which was never recovered. Had he not acted immediately he received my mother's cable I was told, we might have been ruined.

Telepathic communication of this kind is, I believe, fairly common. It certainly existed between me and my mother, whom I adored. What is perhaps less common is a spiritual 'visitation' such as I have described. I have only met two people who have spoken of a similar experience. One of them was my father, who told me Christ visited him in the same way at the age of twelve when he too, badly needed moral support.

CHAPTER II

Home & Parents

My father's childhood had been unhappy. When my grandfather died of pneumonia at the age of 29, he left my grandmother to bring up four small children on very slender means. Even these were partly removed when the Estate was thrown into Chancery as a result of a claim on the property by an Irish relation. To make ends meet my grandmother had to open a boarding house in Brighton, while the children were sent away. My father was sent to an Infant Orphan Asylum where the discipline was fierce and the general atmosphere hostile. My father suffered greatly. When in after years he recalled his experiences at the school he wept. School over, at 14, my father decided he would like to go to sea, but a single voyage on a collier to Norway cured forever his hankering for the nautical life. So he went up to London, as an apprentice to a wholesale textile firm, Pawson & Leaf, whose office until recently was over against St Paul's Cathedral. He was so successful that he was able to leave at 21 to start his own business with a fellow apprentice, Arthur Christopher Denham. Then a strange thing happened. Gordon Selfridge arrived on the London scene from Chicago in 1906, intent on founding a great store to be called Selfridges. One of his first tasks was to set about finding the ideal general manager. He must be trained, full of energy, resourceful, and above all, successful. Extensive inquiries were made. They resulted in an offer to my father which he felt he could not refuse. His partner Denham was sympathetic and perhaps a little relieved not to be permanently second fiddle in their partnership. But before my father could take over at Selfridges two years' construction lay ahead. Meantime Selfridge had become friendly with Sam (afterwards Lord) Waring, whose own business Waring & Gillow was in bad shape. So Selfridge offered to lend my father to Warings for two years and my father took over in 1907 and did a very successful job of reorganisation. At the end of two years my father handed in his resignation saying there was nothing more for him to do. Waring did all he could to dissuade my father from leaving, offering him the managing directorship and a salary of £3,000 (today £135,000) a year. But all to no avail. My father had risen fast and was now restless and successful. He decided to leave the 'retail trade' altogether, as being beneath the notice of a 'gentleman's son.'

So in 1913 my father began an overseas venture, by creating a syndicate of 39 Belgian silk manufacturers for which he was to be sole agent in the U.S.A. On 13 October 1913 we all arrived in New York, to be overtaken nine months later by the Great War . The silk business evaporated and my father was adrift and had to start from the bottom again. This was very hard on my mother, who came from a thoroughly secure, bourgeois Swiss family. Her father Armin Kellersberger was a distinguished lawyer, senator and president of the Swiss Senate. The family lived in Baden. My Swiss grandmother was a Brentano, a family with extensive European connections. All these moves and changes – twenty in their first twenty one years of marriage – were not at all to my mother's liking, but she, in heroic fashion mastered them all without ever losing the charm and beauty which had so attracted my father when he first cast his eye on her.

My parents had met in 1902 when my father was on a walking tour of Switzerland. He was 29, she was 23. My father and his friend Bauer stayed overnight at the Hotel Bulbad in Kandersteg and sat at the long *table d'hôte* opposite the Kellersberger parents and their children. A few words were exchanged, the parents being mildly discouraging as was proper. But before my father left Switzerland he and Lili Kellersberger were engaged, and they married the next year.

Thanks to my father's growing reputation as a company reorganizer – Waring & Gillow, Wanamaker, the Lindell Stores (St Louis) – we became sufficiently well off to be able to return to England. My father found that his English partner A. C. Denham had faithfully maintained their joint business during the 1914-

1918 War. As a result my father was able to retire completely from business in 1926 at the age of 53 and devote his whole energies — which were considerable – to his family and his study of the Bible. He became a convinced believer in the Second Coming of Christ. We were encouraged to believe some dramatic spiritual event would occur on 29 May, 1928, which would usher in the new age. My cousin Anne tells the story that on the preceding night my father went round to see his brother George and urged him to pack. When Uncle George asked why Will thought he would be 'called', my father replied 'because you are a Goyder' as if that were sufficient claim on the next world! This story may be apocryphal but my father was in good company. Emmanuel Swedenborg had dated 'the end of the Age' in 1757, the year of William Blake's birth, and Blake, too, believed in a Second Coming and doubtless took the idea from the writings of Swedenborg.

At Swedenborg House in London there is a portrait of our collateral ancestor the Rev. Thomas Goyder (1786-1849) who was a Swedenborgian bishop (that is to say he was authorised to consecrate clergy of the Swedenborg Persuasion). He wrote a number of Swedenborgian books expounding the Bible, as did the Rev. David George Goyder (1796-1878), Thomas's younger brother. This nonconformist family tradition on my father's side may help to explain my lifelong interest in Swedenborg and William Blake. David George's *Autobiography of a Phrenologist**
tells us about all that is known for certain of the origins of the family, namely that Goyder is Gwydir and the family came from Wales. There is a Gwydir street in Cambridge, and the Welsh Office in Whitehall is Gwydyr House, but our exact family connection with that last surviving bit of unspoiled Georgian architecture in Whitehall cannot with certainty be traced.

What evidence there is seems to come through the Church. The translator of the Welsh Bible, William Morgan, was born in 1541. His father was John ap Morgan a tied tenant of the Wynn

* Simpkin Marshall, London 1857

family, whose ancestral home was Plas Gwydyr. It seems possible that some of the younger members of the Wynn family might have emigrated to England using Gwydyr as their surname, which, when Anglicised became Goyder.

CHAPTER III

Mill Hill School

But I must return to School. The two mystical experiences I have described gave me confidence I had previously lacked. I took the first opportunity to be confirmed, and thereby began a lifelong habit of weekly Holy Communion. My parents bought a house in Mill Hill and in the spring of 1922 I was found a day boy place at Mill Hill School. Two years later I entered as a boarder in School House. Peter Howard was an early friend. As a wing forward I kept him out of the First XV Rugby side in 1925 because the doctors were worried about his withered leg. When the doctors relented, Peter went on to become Captain of Oxford and Captain of England, before taking up from Frank Buchman the leadership of Moral Re-armament.

My particular hero at Mill Hill was Wilfred Sobey, who was destined to be the best English scrum half between the two World Wars. His international fly-half partner Roger Spong captained our House side. These were happy days. I became Junior Gym champion, a member of the school Athletic and Gym teams and the First XV. I also initiated the Model Railway Club which I understand was the earliest but one of its kind in England. I also did some work.

When I entered Mill Hill School the Headmastership was vacant. While a new Headmaster was being chosen to succeed Sir John McClure, discipline at the school suffered. The situation was the reverse of that at Margate College. At Mill Hill elaborate steps were taken by the boys to make the masters' job impossible. One trick I remember was for a boy to bring a live mouse into class and let it loose during a lesson. Everyone then stood on his desk in mock horror and shouted with feigned fright and riotous delight until the unhappy master, who by then was nearly in tears, was driven to try and catch the mouse, to cheers which could be heard all over the school. This effectively disrupted class. It also sent the master concerned into a mental home. But the new headmaster, Mr Maurice Jacks soon put an end to all that. He is said to have beaten half the school in his first term, but this sounds like a slight exaggeration. Certainly order was restored, by methods which the law today might not approve, but which, in a state of war, necessity may dictate.

Being a nonconformist school, Mill Hill had its own Congregational form of Service. But the Anglican parish church was opposite, so I attended Communion there as well as the services in Chapel. It was not a question of piety. Then, as now, I felt I needed all the spiritual help I could get.

I have very happy memories of the masters at Mill Hill who helped direct my steps. It was not so much their teaching that inspired me as the individual enthusiasm of particular masters. Thus Mr Coates talked to us about his passion for astronomy when he was officially teaching mathematics. Mr Whitehead, a man of a stern but lovely character, taught us to behave like gentlemen. E. B. Castle (afterwards Headmaster of Leighton Park School) read us John Ruskin's *Unto This Last* instead of teaching Shakespeare. Ruskin had a profound effect on me. Unemployment in Britain was running at ten percent and there was much gloom in the air. Here, in Ruskin, was a prophet with a vision of human cooperation and economic harmony. I resolved to go into business, find out what was wrong with the system and to try and put it right. A stupid aim? It has influenced and guided my whole life.

CHAPTER IV

Alford House & LSE

A further positive influence was that of Norman Brett James, the
school's deputy headmaster. His encyclopedic knowledge made
history thrilling. He would talk about current affairs with a
politician's enthusiasm. This led me to my first attempt at public
service. The Liberal MP for North Lambeth, Frank Briant, lived
in and ran a Working Men's Club in the Lambeth Walk known as
Alford House (it is still open and busy in nearby Aveline Street).
One day Norman James invited a few of us to meet Frank Briant.
After we had met him I offered to spend my evenings in the Club
while I was at the London School of Economics. Lambeth Walk in
those days was a rough place. The police walked in pairs for self-
protection. Family feuds were frequent, especially on Saturday
nights when the husbands first gathered at the pub and then
continued their arguments in the street, until blows and insults
were exchanged and the wives stood by with hat pins ready to
rescue their man. I am told Lambeth traditionally housed the
servants of the King, as they could readily be ferried over to
Westminster Palace. Their royal connection is said to be the
origin of the cockney's cockiness and irrepressible sense of
humour. Charlie Chaplin and Lupino Lane were both born in
Lambeth. Inspired by Frank Briant, the most Christ-like figure I
had met, I offered to spend six nights of the week in the Club,
sleeping there and going home to my parents on the seventh
night. This I continued doing through 1926 and until February
1930 when I emigrated.

In retrospect Lambeth was as much my university as the
London School of Economics. My father thought working for a
degree a waste of time for someone destined for business. So he
arranged for me to go up to LSE for two instead of three years and
do a double shift, morning and evening, in economics and

politics. I wrote essays for my supervisor, Professor Sargent which were set by Dr Hugh Dalton, head of the economics faculty. One of my essays was a critique of J. A. Hobson's under-consumption theory (in which Hobson was to influence Maynard Keynes). Another dealt with the conservatism of British employers (1927) in face of German competition. In the course of a pessimistic forecast I wrote:

'A primary condition of industrial efficiency is a good relation between employers and workers.'

The search for efficiency in industry and business through cultivation of good human relations was to become my lifelong concern.

At LSE I read widely in the social sciences, listened to Dr Cannan, Professor Gregory and Dr Robbins on economics, Dr Bowley on statistics and Eileen Power on economic history. I stroked the College Boat, played rugby for the First XV, became Assistant Secretary of the Commerce Society and founded the LSE Branch of the Student Christian Movement. When, 25 years later, I was invited to speak at a commemoration dinner at LSE, R. H. Tawney was among the guests of the still active S.C.M. branch.

CHAPTER V

Duke of York's Camp

Another influence was the Duke of York's Camp. For one hectic week in the year, boys from privileged homes and schools and young workers camped together on Romney Marsh. Divided into Sections of 20 boys each, all 400 of us competed fiercely for supremacy in games, competitions and intelligence tests. We thought our Section had a good chance of winning the first prize if only our leader could be made to be less shy. It was not a public school boy but a young Welsh coal miner who solved the problem. He went out on his own and bought some coconuts, stuffed them into our section leader's palliasse, and awaited developments. All shyness disappeared once our Section Leader, who was the future Duke of Hamilton, returned from his late-night briefing session after 'lights out'. Three years later (1928) I was to be a Section Leader myself. To the Duke of York's Camp I owed a precious and lasting friendship with 'Douglo', as the Marquess of Clydesdale was known to his family and friends. Later, when Douglo was the High Commissoner to the General Assembly of the Church of Scotland, we were invited by him and Betty his wife to be their guests at Holyrood. Douglo was a most loveable character and his early death a sadness and a great loss to Scotland.

After my two years at LSE I was ready to start work. But unlike my two brothers, I had no degree or other qualification. My brother Claude was to gain a First in the Mechanical Sciences Tripos at Cambridge, while Cecil was already world famous. Before going to London University, when still a boy at Mill Hill School, Cecil had become the leading amateur radio 'ham' in Britain. A Memorial Tablet at Mill Hill School records his achievement in establishing two-way communication with Australia, U.S.A., China and India, using his own home-made short-wave crystal set. On 18 October 1924 he became the first person ever to achieve round-the-world communication; exchanging greetings with an amateur in New Zealand by the name of Frank Bell. This historic event was front page news in every British newspaper. Sir Edward Appleton, in a BBC publication, describes my brother's feat as:

'The most dramatic single moment in the history of the development of short waves; when the greatest distance possible on this earth was bridged for the first time.'

Cecil had, while still a schoolboy, brought to the school the widest publicity in its history.

In the face of such outstanding achievements what could I do? I felt an urge to offer myself for the Ministry. But having been at school in the U.S.A. from 5 to 12 I knew no Greek and scarcely any Latin – not a good start. All things considered I thought it best to make my way in business, as my father had all along planned, and as I had resolved in 1924 when being read Ruskin's *Unto This Last*.

CHAPTER VI

First Job

My prospects in 1927, when I left LSE, were anything but rosy. Unemployment was running at ten percent of the insured population and increasing. (It was to average fourteen percent between the Wars.) So I took the first job I was offered, which came through an American acquaintance of my father's. I joined a company which owned a paper agency and a small paper mill, the latter in the South of France.

After six weeks in the London office I was shipped out to their French subsidiary. My fellow workers warned me that the policy of the firm was 'catch 'em young, tell 'em nothing, and ship 'em off abroad' which was to be exactly my experience.

My pay in London was £7 a month. But while in France I would be paid 1,000 francs a month or £96 per year. It was understood that board and lodging would be provided, so I could be a few pounds better off. But when I received my first French pay cheque, there was no allowance for board or lodging. I had been given a reduction – not an increase – in pay.

I lived in a small house in the village. One day I came home at midday to find an endless stream of white ants had made a passage to my kitchen. Ants could be expelled. A more difficult problem was that the postmistress regularly steamed open incoming letters, so that the village knew their contents before the addressees! We never did find out what happened to the outgoing post! When I inquired innocently about someone's past, I was told to forget it. Practically everyone in the village had a criminal record and it was considered bad form to refer to the past.

We worked round the clock in twelve hour shifts, although this was illegal. When the Gendarmerie periodically surrounded the factory on horseback, all work instantly reverted to the statutory eight hours. Anyone telling the truth would have been sacked next day.

One Friday – pay day – I sat at my desk at lunch with the manager opposite. In walked a bulky French worker and demanded to see the patron about his pay. The Manager signed to me to keep my head down. Neither of us moved. The worker produced a rifle and pointed it at my head from about six feet. After some mutterings the angry worker left the room and fired off his gun outside the office. In that way he could show his wife and colleagues that he had carried out his threat, without actually hurting anybody.

Another time our French clerk failed to return from motor bicycling to Bergerac where he collected the wages fortnightly from the bank. He had been mugged and robbed but was not seriously hurt.

We made guncotton from cotton linters which was sold to the French and Polish governments. A side line was handmade paper, including toilet paper bearing the monograms of royal personages. One day the Poudrerie at Angouleme blew up – whether due to a high copper number in our guncotton or someone else's we were not told; but there was considerable loss of life and thereafter what went into the vats was very closely controlled.

My father came out, and after sizing up the situation wrote a letter to the two managers, reading as follows:

'You are in foreign exile (not anglo-saxon) in a small, poor, isolated French village, deprived of the spiritual, moral, and physical advantages of British civilized life such as church, friends, and homes provide, with the nearest town too far away to be any relief to the monotony of your lives. You have not even water fit to drink, alcoholic drink becoming compulsory. You are thrown so closely together in your daily lives that you are entirely dependent upon one another, in itself a well known danger and source of irritation. No society, no relaxation, no games, no amusements, not even reasonable comfort or properly furnished rooms. Your housekeeping is poorly done for you, though in France good cooking is almost universal. I have asked myself if these things are necessary or excusable under the circumstances, for poverty alone can justify them. I find they are not. Your London employers are wealthy and prosperous. Their business is very profitable and the return on the capital invested is, I judge, unusually high. Therefore their first duty and pleasure should be to make the conditions of their young men employees as acceptable as possible. It would call for a comparatively trifling sum from the large profits to put the deteriorated tennis court into playing condition, to provide water fit to drink, to furnish and decorate the living rooms decently and brightly, to supply a few books and papers from home etc. Some show of consideration and sense of responsibility is the plain duty of employers. Instead, I find a callous neglect of your welfare and a total disregard of the possible spiritual, moral, or physical deterioration which might be expected from such conditions.In addition, the hours of work are unlimited. Always under-staffed, you are forced to work 12 to 15 hours a day and 7 days a week, a condition which cannot be too severely criticized. Sunday working has been condemned by all efficiency investigations both with men and beasts. It was not for nothing that it was forbidden by Divine Law – and British civil law. Promises for the future are offered, and are considered the chief incentive, and also the sacrifices and self-abnegation of such a life are urged as being for young men an ideal worthy of their submission. (The learner was told that "he would be judged by his power of endurance.") This may be. One year would prove it, and it can be judged by its fruits. But I have noticed that three years of the manager will have become 'future' without result. Also, continual promises of withdrawal end in continual stay in Couze, from which the difficulty of escape without discharge is obvious. And if the "ideal" or "test of manhood" of living under such conditions, needless as they are, ends in deterioration, discharge is quite definitely promised. And in France of all countries! In my very varied and wide experiences as an organizer in England and America, with large staffs up to 2,000 in my care, I have not heard an example of employers

17

so ungenerous in recognising their responsibilities to young men serving them in a foreign country, or who paid them so badly.

William Goyder'

After this letter it was clear that I should have to resign and the only question was when. We agreed to wait until my visit home in August, when I walked into the office and told the director the reasons for which I had decided not to return. After hearing my story he asked me to wait. Some minutes elapsed, then I was ushered into the boardroom and informed by the chairman that I was sacked!

CHAPTER VII

At Spicers

Now good fortune intervened. Through Norman Brett James an introduction was arranged by my father to Sir Albert Spicer, a governor of Mill Hill School and chairman of Spicers, paper merchants in New Bridge Street. As a result of his intervention I was interviewed by the company secretary and received a letter engaging me for their export department at £2 a week to start on 21 August 1928. This was my first increase in pay and I worked within a stones' throw of my first employers.

The next eighteen months was to be a period of consolidation. I lived during the week in Lambeth Walk and worked at Alford House in the evening. By day I was learning about paper in all its forms. I went to classes at the London School of Printing. After a year I was moved into the Export Manager's office where I could listen to the manager's handling of telephone inquiries. In August I asked for a rise and was put up from £2 to £5 a week. But I was preparing myself for a complete break. I had conceived the idea of going to America to seek my fortune. I was torn between a desire to serve Christ in some meaningful capacity and of pursuing a business career for which my conviction, training, and my father's influence, had prepared me. By emigrating I thought I should be placing myself under Divine guidance, which I knew I should need.

My father had taught me to treat personal saving as an essential preliminary to a career in business. One's first £100 was to be the passport to economic liberty, and a goal to be striven for. (Today it would be nearly £3,000). So in my monthly accounts, saving received top priority. I still have a small, leather-bound book containing my accounts from my entry into business in 1928 until 1940. The entry for March 1928 reads as follows:

INCOME F.Francs		EXPENDITURE	
Opening balance	635.55	Savings	360.00
Pay	1000.00	Board & Lodging	617.00
		Books	120.00
		Washing	30.00
		Stamps	25.00
		all other	46.00
			1,198.00
		balance in hand	437.55
			1,635.55

Treating savings – including the tithe – as a prior running expense may be unorthodox bookkeeping, but it is a continual reminder of the importance of looking forward. In this way, tithing became a habit and a lifelong expression of gratitude.

CHAPTER VIII

To America

While at Couze I had saved 2,136 francs (£17) out of a total income of 6,600 francs. When, eighteen months later, I sailed for America to seek my fortune, I had accumulated savings of £82. To this my father added £100, but before leaving England I had to buy my passage on the *George Washington*. She was a cabin class steamship which meant that I travelled First Class for £35. I spent a similar sum on clothes, so I arrived in New York on 1 March, 1930 with $525 of capital. I reckoned this would be enough to sustain me for six or seven weeks, provided my expenditure was kept to a bare minimum.

When saying goodbye, my father had accompanied his gift with a piece of advice and a letter of introduction to his old business partner Dr Kubler. The latter told me to take the next boat home. He thought I could never get a job in the slump following the Wall Street crash. My father's advice was different. Seeing there would be thousands of young Americans looking for work at a time of deep depression, he thought I should be wise to make myself familiar with the business atmosphere in the U.S.A. before trying to persuade someone to employ me. It was good advice and I took it. But first I rented a room at the Allerton House on 55th Street, a sort of YMCA, where a room cost only $12 a month and lunch 50¢. That Sunday, after church, I visited the Farlows, old friends of the family, and there met the man who became my greatest friend – Dana Kelley. He worked with Bankers' Trust, had lost money in the Wall Street crash, and was trying, sadly with the help of the bottle, to recover himself. In spite of the Prohibition Laws, alcohol was freely available, but I never touched it. Although he joined Alcoholics Anonymous, Dana died in his late fifties. There could not have been a kinder, more thoughtful, more courteous gentleman. He and his lovely wife

Priscilla Robineau kept me sane in New York and helped me to hold loneliness at bay. I could always rely on spending an evening with them and their small son in their comfortable apartment. I think Dana never fully recovered from the Wall Street crash. He was too sensitive to brush it aside, and too committed to leave Wall Street. He ended his career as a respected vicepresident of Bankers' Trust.

On Thursday (6 March, 1930), I set off on the great adventure. The log of my journey covers Philadelphia, Baltimore, Washington, Pittsburgh, Akron, Cleveland, Detroit, Buffalo, Erie and New York, or seven out of the U.S.A.'s ten largest industrial cities. When I got back to New York on 5 April, I had $300 left. That meant I had to get myself a job in a week or ten days. The fact that if I failed I might then not have enough money to return home did not occur to me at the time, although it has since. On my travels I met a great many people and made some valuable business connections.

In Philadelphia, my cousin Laurence Le Page, designer of the Pitcairn Autogiro (Cierva), took me on a flight over the city. He also made me write down on a single sheet what qualifications I had that might interest a prospective employer. A surprising collection of hidden talents emerged from this exercise, and this gave me confidence.

On board the *George Washington* I had been 'adopted' by two distinguished middle aged men who invited me to join them. One, Mr J. T. Williams was editor of the *Christian Science Monitor*, *persona grata* at the White House and formerly Hearst's political editor. With him was Sir Basil Clarke, one of Northcliffe's editors whose extempore rendering of the Londonderry Air on the ship's piano made me feel exactly like the emigrant I was! Mr Williams put me up at the Cosmos Club in Washington, took me to the U.S. Senate to hear a debate on foreign policy, and next day went with me by car to Mount Vernon to visit George Washington's home. He was kindness itself.

On my way to Washington I had the only serious incident in all my travels in the U.S.A. I never told my parents about it. It was

6p.m. and growing dark when I arrived at Baltimore to stay the night and go on to Washington next day. Someone, whom I took to be a porter, grabbed my suitcase at the station and ran off with it past the taxi rank and on to a dilapidated 'hotel' beyond. There was no-one around except for two evil looking men who pushed the hotel register at me and told me to sign it. I went upstairs and found my bedroom had doors on three sides of the room and there was no way of locking any of them. I came downstairs feeling trapped and knew I must get out at all costs. Not knowing what to do I crossed the street and re-entered the station. I heard a low hiss. It was repeated. I looked about. A coloured man behind the cloakroom desk whispered 'Get out of there, get out fast or you will be robbed and worse'. He was clearly terrified of being over-heard. I understood him, immediately walked back to the 'hotel', collected my bag, came down to the desk and said 'I have just received a telegram and must go on', saying which I walked boldly out of the door followed by two pairs of hostile and evil eyes. I quickly hailed a cab and said 'Drive to the Stadler Hotel'. It was a close shave and I hope my lie will be forgiven. I think that negro attendant risked his life for me.

In the U.S.A. introductions are – or were – given gladly and generously. This made meeting people easy.

From Toronto I wrote my parents (30 March):
'One chance connection I hardly thought of taking up gave me a letter to a man in the Hanover Trust. His secretary gave me one to four people, two of them in banks in Detroit. One of these gave me four intros. to people in Detroit. Had I not had them my card would have been almost blank. As it was I got to the President of one of the big refrigerator concerns.'

It was Kelvinator, and they offered me a job. Not having transport was sometimes a problem.

TUESDAY 25 MARCH (Detroit). Arrived at 6.30 a.m. (from Cleveland) in a snowstorm. Followed up two intros. to bank officials and spent afternoon getting to Ford Airport. Saw Mr Stout, the President of Ford Aircraft, and arranged for

Thursday. He took me back to Detroit in his car. Spent evening in my room, and was grateful for the Stadler radio. A fine Hotel.

WEDNESDAY 26 (Detroit). Still snowing. Spent whole day getting to Ford's and back. Detroit is an impossible place to get round in without a car.

WEDNESDAY 2 APRIL (Buffalo). Followed up two intros. to Buffalonians. The first took me to lunch and fixed me up at his club, the best in Buffalo. I took a room there and moved out of the hotel. Was introduced to eminent men of the City, including Pres. of the Chamber of Commerce, who arranged to have me visit the chief factories next day.

THURSDAY 3 APRIL (Buffalo, contd.) Spent day going over Stewart Motor Truck Co., Ontario Biscuit Co., and Dunlops of America, all with an escort from the Chamber of Commerce by car. Chatted with the presidents of the first two of these concerns. A busy and interesting day.'

I arrived back in New York on Saturday 5 April. My financial position had deteriorated but the experience had been invaluable. I still had $300 and reckoned it enough for a week or ten days. On Monday (7 April) I started my job hunt in earnest. On my travels I had opened eighteen business connections and in the week of 7-11 April made a dozen more. It was hard work, as the following letter to my parents shows:

'Allerton House, N.Y.
13 April (Sunday)

I have had an enormously busy week. I have worked without a single stop all day for the last week interviewing people. It is tiring work because you have to be thinking and planning all the time. This coming week will be the same... I have had lunch with someone every day last week and I hope to continue! While I can get free lunches I don't need a job!'

When the week was over I had lined up four jobs that were attractive and I still had to see International Paper. This was the decisive interview, and led to a job for life. I went along on Monday morning and met Mr Richard Doane, the export manager. He asked me a great many questions and then offered me a job in his office. I accepted at once. Nothing had been said about my salary, so rather hesitatingly I asked what it would be. 'What you have asked.' Dr Kubler had told me to ask for $100 a month. I tripled that in my application and I was now on $300 a month: riches! I can't say what appealed to me so much about Mr Doane. He had an extraordinary habit. All the time he talked to me a large cigar was revolving in his mouth. Gradually it was disappearing until finally only a small stub was left. I was fascinated and couldn't keep my eyes off the cigar.

What of the jobs I didn't take? Hammermill Paper wanted me to go to Australia for them. International General Electric would have taken me as a refrigerator salesman and sent me to Europe. Mr Firstbrook (Toronto) introduced me to Victor Donaldson who had just been brought from Canada to be President of the Robert Gair Company, and one of the largest U.S.A. packaging businesses. It occurred to me that coming from outside to head an established business he would need a personal assistant whose only loyalty would be to himself. After thinking it over for a couple of days Mr Donaldson offered me that job. The fourth offer was to join Duponts in their cellophane branch. The production manager was willing to engage me but needed the authority of his sales manager. Before this came I was already committed to International Paper. When I told the other three companies each said: 'If things don't work out come back and see us again.' I had from the start made Easter my deadline and the job with International Paper came through on April 17, the day before Good Friday. I had just $85 left. Writing to my parents on Easter Monday I summed up my feelings:

'I returned to NY with 18 connections... I was offered a job by virtually everyone I went to although Kubler knew that I had been unlucky enough to hit the worst depression in America since 1920... the way things moved to success was positively uncanny. If I had gone on for another week I should have had a dozen jobs to choose from… therefore I closed my business within ten days owing to rush of orders! I am taking this week off in which to forget the whole business and get myself into a "beginner" frame of mind.'

It had been an extraordinary experience in which I felt a strong sense of Providence. There was something beyond the ordinary about it which time alone could unravel. It was as if I had an unseen personal helper who could direct events beyond my reckoning or capacity.

CHAPTER IX

International Paper Company

My business career in U.S.A. began on 28 April 1930. when I started work as one of five office boys in the head office of the International Paper Co. in New York. We delivered mail to the desks in the sales department and simultaneously collected mail for re-delivery. It was a way of quickly getting to know everyone in the office. There were about 100 in the department and they were on several floors. But there was a snag. I was being paid at least three times the rate for the job. How could I earn my keep? The answer proved simple: run. So I ran all day for a week from desk to desk, from floor to floor, hardly ever sitting down except at lunch time. I had been a long distance runner at school so the exercise did me no harm.

Nonetheless, I was glad when after a week I was given a desk in the export department. Now I sat facing a frosted glass partition behind which was Mr Richard Doane who had engaged me. He was a man wholly devoted to the business. At 33 he was already the Export Sales Manager reporting direct to the President and Vice President of the sales company.

IP produced every type of paper and board and the company's production exceeded the whole of Britain's annual consumption. The company was also the largest landowner in North America apart from the U.S.A. and Canadian governments, the sixth largest producer of power in U.S.A., and the owner of several newspapers. At the time I joined IP was selling one quarter of the newsprint used in the U.S.A. Under the leadership of the President, Archibald Graustein, a lawyer of fabulous reputation and a dynamic personality, IP had expanded rapidly into Canada where both the raw material and power was on the doorstep. Having built the world's largest paper mill at Three Rivers, and equally modern mills at Gatineau and New Brunswick, the company was in a very strong competitive position. But newsprint mills are always vulnerable because the percentage capital cost is greater than in any other industry except steel. When demand falls off and the mills have to go on short time, losses can mount up very rapidly. A modern paper mill needs to operate at 70% or more of its capacity, or it will fail.

As an 'executive apprentice' I was taken to the port of New York to see one of our paper ships unloaded (with paper for the New York Times) and then into the *New York World*, *Herald Tribune* and *New York Times* pressrooms where the paper was being used. I was told this was a rare privilege and to say absolutely nothing. Mr Doane next arranged for me to go to Canada and see newsprint being made at the Three Rivers Mill. They did not normally admit visitors. After a strenuous week in the Mill (at temperatures well over 90°F) I returned to New York.

My next assignment was to go to Orono, Maine, for six weeks to attend the University of Maine Summer School on paper technology, all expenses being paid by the company. Mr Doane asked me to write a weekly report. I was glad to be able to record the highest marks of the course – 97 and 100% – and received a letter of congratulation from Mr Fearing the Vice President on winning the University Tennis Tournament (my only-ever success in a tennis tournament). On 18 August I returned to New York. I was thunderstruck by what followed. I was called into Mr Doane's office, the door shut, and told that I had been appointed personal assistant to Mr Doane in place of Mr Henry Cullen, who had been transferred elsewhere. (We became good friends afterwards and remained so until Henry's death.) Mr Cullen was said to have 'lacked initiative'. That evening Mr Doane outlined the job to me: I was to take as much as possible of the routine management off his hands so as to give him time to think and plan and visit. He would pass all the work to me that I could absorb.

It didn't seem possible to have become a member of the executive team four months after joining the company. I was taken aback. Here is an extract from the letter I wrote my parents that night (23 August):

'I expect you were rather surprised at the last part of my letter last week to you, about my new work... IP are very anxious to expand in the export trade... my hope all along has been to return to England in some capacity for them, and perhaps in time to be their European representative... Also there had to be something to justify the way they were treating me. I have spent four months wondering what would happen to me when I finished my course of training... but I must admit I have got more than I ever bargained for... the first day Doane didn't send for me or speak to me, or the next day. I began wondering what he expected me to do. I had received no instructions. He had been so busy that he obviously had no time to give me. He worked till 7 p.m. on Tuesday and 8.30 p.m. Wednesday... When I got in on Thursday I found several things put on my desk to be done, letters to answer and memoranda to write. This kept me busy most of the day. I found no difficulty in handling Doane's correspondence and he made no comments on the letters I gave him for signing... but I still felt unsettled, not knowing exactly what my new job meant, yet feeling that it ought to mean quite a lot.

I stayed in on Thursday, waiting to show Doane some files. He called me in at 6.30 and began to talk to me. He talked until after 8 p.m. He sat back in his chair and just talked quietly without stopping. He described the work of his department, the business of selling newsprint, the difficulties, the reason why we were not making money, the international politics of the newsprint game. Then he told me what his job was, and what it involved, and what my job was to be and what it involved. His talk was unlike anything I had ever heard. He didn't try at all to be careful – he just gave me the straight truth in a fine, clear, and very kind and human way. It really thrilled me, though I didn't say so. I had all along suspected and been told by others that Doane is the coming man in IP. His fingers are on everything... He surveys the whole world newsprint situation... I describe the set-up so that you can understand the picture as it affects me.

To return to Doane's talk... he talked clearly and without restraint. He told me exactly what I was here for and what he

wanted me to do, and how I was to do it and how I was to fit in with him. He ended by saying "I am the only man in the company who understands the business in all its manifestations. I want you to learn all I know, and more." Finally he said he wanted me to be able to take over from him so that he can move around, a week here, two weeks there, or to England for a month.'
I went on:

'I am disappointed because I cannot see myself back in England this year – or next. I look at it this way. In the nature of things I had to go away in order to stand on my own feet. I grudge losing a year or two – precious years with you – but I do feel full of confidence that these very years will be made up to us. Of course I am driving at the fact that nothing can compensate for the years spent away from you – except for the future with you. I never have reconciled myself to being permanently away from you, and I don't now. My coming here was a gamble, and you let me go gladly and put nothing in the way., I gambled too, on being back in England within a year, though I didn't tell you so… well, I have lost my gamble for the time being, but lost it to win a better. To sum it up, there are just two opportunities in IP which reconcile me to living here a year or two (1) assistant to the President (2) assistant to Mr Doane, and I have the second.'

While all this was going on I moved out of town to a N.Y. suburb, New Rochelle, and to a room in the home of Mrs Quinn, a devout and splendid Catholic woman with three boys, whose father had died recently leaving the family in poor circumstances. The address was 192 Woodland Avenue, only a few minutes' walk from 163 Meadow Lane where we had lived after my parents' return from St Louis and where I had attended Trinity School to High School grade.

I liked all the Quinn family. The room I rented was comfortable and the rent was $9 a week, so I was able to save rapidly. During the first four months I earned $1,200 and spent $536. I was saving half my income and steadily building up capital. The Quinn boys liked having a man in the house and at weekends we could go down to Long Island Sound together, swim and generally enjoy the beauty of New Rochelle. When I wanted a change I could always stay with the Kelleys in their N.Y. apartment. My parents' friends, the Farlows, lived opposite Trinity School. Through them I met George Gillette, a shy man some ten years older than I was and suspicious of all young females because of his great wealth. He owned the Gillette Safety Razor Company. I would go to a show or the opera with him. Then back to his Park Avenue mansion opposite the Pierpont Morgans' home and into a comfortable four poster in which I could do better than dream of being a millionaire. For the time I was one! I also made friends in New Rochelle. One of them, Nelda Harrison, a lovely young woman with a good husband and two small daughters, fell in love with me. It was embarrassing. On the spur of the moment I persuaded her to go with me to church and say our prayers together and then go and talk it out with her husband. We did this and remained friends, although from then on we saw less of each other. Nelda gave me a copy of Emily Dickinson's poems in which she wrote:

'To George –
Never bud from a stem
stepped with so gay a foot,
Never a worm so confident
Bored at so brave a root'

If I got through this episode without disaster it was only because of my convictions and the example of my parents.

On 7 September I wrote as follows:

'Another busy week has gone by. I work late every night and get away at 7.30 p.m. on the average. When I have had dinner there is time for little except bed. But it is all for the good. My work is all important just now... Doane is so busy that I get only a few minutes with him a day.

Far from being bullish, for the past month or more everyone here is plunged in extreme pessimism, and this has lately penetrated the up to now imperviously optimistic spirit of IP. Hence as I warn you, anything may happen.'

(2 0 S E P T E M B E R) Every day convinces me that I have an extraordinary opportunity... Doane and Graustein are the two members of TICON – The International Committee on Newsprint – from IP. This is a committee of all the American mills which is trying to stabilise the industry... Can you wonder that I work late every night... or that Doane works till 8-9 p.m. almost every night.

(3 0 S E P T E M B E R) Wall Street is very gloomy – the whole situation has blackened to a surprising degree at the very time a revival was due.

(2 6 O C T O B E R) The newsprint industry is in a critical state, and pending the merger of all the interests in a central cartel all our stocks have sunk – Abitibi preferred has gone from 85 to 35 while ours from 80 to 45. The paper industry has only worked at 65% capacity this year. 180,000 tons of new capacity will absorb all the increase there is likely to be in 1931.

I am tremendously impressed with the way IP do business. It coincides as nearly as I could expect with my ideal of efficient management... Doane has the right outlook. He never assumes he is right, nor lets anyone else. He expects everyone to know the facts – all of them – and he expects you to get things done. I attend to all the detail work I can without speaking to him. I just do the job and hope it will be good enough to earn his confidence.

(2 N O V E M B E R) I have joined the Speakers Training Division of the Advertising Club of New York. Every Thursday I go from 5.30 to 10 p.m. and make a short speech each time to 50 other business men who are all anxious to improve their public presence.' [I came third in the subsequent speaking competition. First and second went to veteran speakers so I was first in the beginners' group.]

We sell 40,000 tons a year of newsprint in England. Mr Doane called me in on Thursday and put me in charge. If I handle it well I shall automatically be the Company's Export Manager. I shall also be handling our 6,000 tons a year Australian business and in New Zealand. It is now 10 p.m. and I have to outline a suggested organisation to him and I must make it up as I go along – if I work all night it doesn't matter, for Tuesday is a whole holiday.

In my room in New Rochelle I now have a piano on which to practise.

(9 NOVEMBER) Another week gone by, so quickly that it was hardly noticed. I am so bound up in my work that time seems to have lost all meaning, and before I can realise it I shall be home again. Make no mistake – Europe is the only place for me. All this struggle isn't worth it unless I have that to look forward to. Sometimes America gets on your nerves ... in spite of meaning so well it somehow offends all the aesthetic senses. It is built round the idea that business is first and last, and such a picayune philosophy is bound to make one restless – to me America's saving grace is its people.'

About this time I began a custom of playing squash after business hours with Hobie Peck who was in a similar position to mine and ended his career as president of Canadian IP. After tiring ourselves out we would adjourn to Childs Restaurant where for 75¢ we could eat anything and everything on the menu. We usually were content with a fish and two meat dishes, but when it came to the sweet course we would order half a dozen dishes each, and the same with the *hors d'oeuvres*. We kept the score and could as a rule eat between two and three times the 75¢. Not surprisingly, this arrangement came to an end once the worst of the depression had passed.

There was better news to end the year. I wrote:

(17 DECEMBER 1930) 'We are holding the price up and believe we shall succeed in avoiding a price war ... lower price would have been suicide and most publishers (newspapers) realise it. But 1931 will be a critical year. If not price cuts, there will be ruthless competition for tonnage. Doane sails for England Jan. 15th.'

He had decided to cross the Atlantic to see Lord Beaverbrook, leaving me in charge of the company's export sales of newsprint. In the event, by negotiating a new long term agreement with

Express Newspapers Doane was able to stabilise a demoralised North American newsprint market. His departure gave me my opportunity and I now met the legendary president of the Company Mr Graustein, and briefed Doane on the British position in a night session before he left. I ended 1930 homesick but reconciled.

(26 JANUARY 1931)'I have been through the busiest week I ever had. First of all I had to get Doane safely off to England. I worked all last Sunday and achieved an analysis of the English business for Doane which ought I think to please him. I breathed a sigh of relief when he had gone and the enormous job of thinking of all he would need was over... But the excitement only began when Doane left. The next day Beaverbrook – who is trying to get out of his contract with us and is employing the finest legal minds in England as advisers to this end – sent Graustein a cable which looked innocent but which would result in our being caught in a very awkward situation if we answered in two of the three obvious ways.

Mr Fearing sent the cable in for me to draft a reply (to my great surprise). I of course drafted a wire to Doane on the Bremen and an alternative direct to Beaverbrook. Fearing wouldn't wait for a reply from Doane and sent my cable up to Graustein and it was sent off. But the exciting thing was that in my cable I had avoided the danger point – mention of it would likely cause our contracts to be voided – and Fearing stuck the very thing in, which I had avoided. As you know he is the first vice-president and sales manager, and I have always been very careful and kept away from him because he is one of the hardest men imaginable to handle, and will trip you up if he can, and do it ruthlessly.

However, I knew my ground this time, and caution went to the winds for I was anxious enough about the cable not to care about Fearing. I told him I thought he was making a mistake, and proved it to him. After a little argument he altered the cable to read as I had proposed ... he has since been very nice and has several times called me into his office and asked me things.

Yesterday another cable came in, cleverer and much more

difficult than the first one. It was Saturday p.m. when we got it. The cable involved our whole contractual obligations with Beaverbrook and is extraordinarily difficult to answer... I had ten minutes to study my facts. Then Fearing took me up with him to the President's office. I waited, and to my great relief Fearing came out and said we could have till Monday to reply, and I didn't have to go in and explain something to the President which I don't know much about. When I make my bow to him I want to be prepared.

But Fearing took me downstairs to his office and we drafted a report to Graustein on it. Then he asked me to suggest a reply, and I declined. I am very glad I did. I am not, and told him I wasn't, competent to suggest a reply. I think, on thinking it over, that I did the best and only thing in the circumstances. But you know how these big men are – think you *must* be able to answer any question they ask. Perhaps he was only asking to see if I would make the mistake of trying to be clever. If so he didn't get a rise out of me that time. There is a great deal of excitement going on because the Australian situation is also critical, and it is almost impossible to get money out of the country.'

During these negotiations I spent an evening with the Kelleys and was taken by George Gillette to see Ruth Draper and wrote 'she is wonderful, her art is finished'. So it was not all work, but in a sense all play. A week earlier I had written:

'My heart is not here at all, and has no greater pleasure than to look forward to being a European again when I have done what's necessary here.'

Writing a few days later I returned to the subject.

15 FEBRUARY 1931 'However much I like it here, I don't, and mustn't forget what I am here for, to suck all the experience from this crazy business civilisation that I can get, preparing myself for bigger work later on in Europe ... as things stand today, almost exactly a year since I left you, I find myself coming upon a door of great opportunity in business – having already in one year gained experience that could not have come my way in many years, work in Europe. I have fallen into an opportunity

that I could only dream of before coming out here. Here I find myself at a place where the greatest paper company in the world is seeking to expand in world markets ... if the export situation develops it is just the field which will use all the training I have had – languages, good general knowledge, experience of two export companies already established.

I look forward most to coming back to Europe. After all, if business is one's career it should mean more than money (I have little ambition to ever be an American business king) and what else it means and will mean in time to come is summed up in organisation of the community for purposes of production – different, more logical, more Christian ways of organising material activity. (Europe, not America, will, I think, be the birthplace of the new civilisation, the new method, and I want to be on hand for that. I am more interested in that than in pursuing a simple money making career.) That will be the great adventure of the next 20 years. I long for it.

You can readily see that there is a causal sequence in the Duke of York's Camp; Alford House; America. It has given birth to an idea, or rather the idea came into being while I was at LSE, that business would be a worthwhile career if it was approached in the same spirit a man should approach his ordination to the Church. All the rest is in the working out. It seems a long long way off now, but I want you to know what is in my mind ... a year over here has led me to believe the vision is not so impossible after all.'

On his return from his successful journey to England Doane began to lean on me more and more. He told me to take over the drafting of a contract with an Australian company whose head man came from Sydney to make an agency agreement with us. The lawyers altered two phrases but approved my draft. I also drew up a fresh English contract, in spite of having no legal training. I learnt as I went along. My first English contract – with Southern Newspapers, Southampton, went through without a question being raised. But there was no time for complacency. On 3 April I wrote my parents, 'Every day one ends dissatisfied. The job is limitless. One always is short of time, short of experience, short of thinking power.'

Increasingly the depression was taking its toll. The Minnesota Paper Co. (M & O) was in receivership, our rivals in Canada on the verge of collapse and unable to pay bond interest. The continuing decline of the market and the general atmosphere of pessimism was heightened by the unbelievable fall in share values.

On 3 September 1929, just six months before I arrived in New York, the U.S. Stock Market had reached an all time peak. Then it collapsed. The decline was catastrophic. By 1932, 'the cruellest year', General Motors' shares – the number one U.S. company – had fallen from 72 to 7, General Electric from 396 to 34, and U.S. Steel from 261 to 21. Millions had been borrowed from the U.S. banks to buy stocks on margin. The result was financial chaos, ending in the closure of the U.S. banks on 4 March 1933. For the next ten days we each printed and circulated our own paper giving our name, address and the amount, and these bits of paper were accepted and exchanged freely as currency.

It takes some imagination to comprehend the magnitude of the disaster – wages down 60%, salaries 40%, farm incomes down from $12 billion in 1929 to $5 billion in 1932. And the human cost was incalculable. A million transients seeking work – any work, unemployment rising from 3 to 6 million in 1930, from 6 to 10 million in 1931, and from 10 to 13 million in 1932. In Buffalo, one of the cities I visited on my job hunt, the unemployment rate in 1932 reached 30%.

The 'Great Crash' affected everyone in America. In less than three years it blew away a sum equal to twice the national debt or nearly the whole of the expenditure by the U.S.A. on the first World War. In Europe it led to Britain going off gold and in Germany to 7 million unemployed and to Adolf Hitler. We were very fortunate in International Paper to suffer only a 10% cut in salaries.

CHAPTER X

Return to England

It was now high summer and a full year had passed since I had set out to seek my fortune. For the first time I became depressed by the growing hopelessness of the American scene and felt a strong sense of loss. Staying with the Kelleys had been my moral support during the first year. Now in July and in the discomfort of being baked in a great heat, I felt dispirited. Dana Kelley was kindness itself and while Priscilla and young Dana were away in the country I stayed with Dana in New York. He was an agnostic and inclined to scoff gently. When I told him I was in a mood of despair and therefore positive that Providence would show itself, he discounted my conviction.

Just three weeks after this failure of nerve (the first since I had left England) I was called in to see Fearing and Doane. Without preliminaries Fearing said: 'We want you to go to England for us. How soon can you leave?'

I nearly jumped out of my skin, but held on and answered: 'The *Majestic* sails tomorrow at midnight.' 'Can you catch her?' asked Fearing. 'Yes,' was my reply. And I did.

The contrast between a life of hard and unremitting work in New York's sticky climate and having one's dinner jacket laid out on one's bed in a first class cabin on a luxury liner was something I shall never forget. Providence had intervened at the critical moment. In London I put up at the Grosvenor House Hotel where I had a suite. I was now the overseas representative of a great company with a status to maintain.

My instructions were to make as many contacts with British newspaper executives as possible and endeavour to persuade them to buy their newsprint from Canada as well as from Sweden, Norway, Finland and the British home mills. This involved considerable travelling, but I was usually able to spend weekends with my parents at Walton-on-Thames. In October Doane came over to see how I was doing, and we visited newspapers together. He seemed pleased, without saying much, and we returned together to New York in November. I had been living in New Rochelle, but now that I was working so closely with Doane I decided to spend the winter in New York and took a ground level flat in Greenwich Village on 10th Street at a rent of $70 a month. Cockroaches abounded, but I negotiated a treaty not to disturb them so long as they kept off my bed, which contract they kept!

But I was soon to be needed in England again: business was still falling away and our newsprint mills were desperate for orders. Canadian newsprint production fell by 25% between 1929 and 1933.

In the Spring of 1932 I sailed from New York on the *S.S. Mauritania*, which had, after twenty-five years active service, regained the Blue Riband from the *S.S. Bremen*. On the voyage I made a friendship which was to be lifelong. Michael Huxley was returning with his family from the U.S.A. intending to resign his post and his prospects in the diplomatic service in order to start a new magazine devoted to geography. The weather was warm, and we sat for hours on deck discussing the future. The company on board the *Mauritania* was overwhelmingly British, and it was rather like being a member of an exclusive English club. On the last day of our voyage – spent largely with the Huxleys – I received a telegram asking me to telephone New York the moment I landed. I showed it to the Purser who showed it to the Captain who telephoned the Manager of the Southern Railway who agreed to stop the boat train at Walton-on-Thames where my parents lived so that I might lose no time in telephoning New York. I was pretty certain it would be something to do with Lord Beaverbrook, and it was. I then telephoned my mother and asked her to be at the station at a certain time when she would have a surprise. She was alone on the platform (apart from the station-master) when the all-Pullman boat train pulled up at Walton Station for one brash young person to alight and greet his mother. What gall! I cannot imagine doing the same thing today, but in those days anything seemed possible.

CHAPTER II

Round the World

In June my salary was raised to $5,000 a year and at the same time I was instructed to go as soon as possible to Australia and New Zealand in search of further newsprint contracts. Our newsprint mills were operating at only 70% of capacity and fresh orders had become a matter of corporate survival. So I took the *Mauritania* again, this time from Southampton and arrived in New York in time to catch the N.Y. Chicago '20th Century Limited', the best known express train in the U.S.A. I planned to sail on the *S.S. Mariposa* leaving in a few days from San Francisco for Honolulu, Samoa, Fiji, New Zealand and Australia. Unfortunately our locomotive developed a hot box in the Salt Lake Desert, where we remained a night and a day in considerable discomfort until relief came. Meantime the *Mariposa* had sailed. But I found there was a 'plane to Los Angeles, so I caught my ship there. Then followed a blissful month at sea with nothing to do but eat, sleep and bathe. What impressed me most was to see a school of sharks tearing a great whale to shreds in heavy weather in the Tasman Sea.

In Australia I had the good fortune to meet Keith Murdoch of the *Melbourne Herald*. He and his wife invited me to spend several days at their beautiful home near Melbourne while we were negotiating a newsprint contract. I was taken to the Melbourne Races and introduced to many of Keith's friends, including Thorold Fink whose father owned the paper. I still have a photograph I took of Rupert Murdoch aged three together with his sister. Rupert already looks quite determined.

Ian Bowater was also in Melbourne, hoping to land a newsprint contract for his family firm, but Keith Murdoch kept us both on tenterhooks. This went on until finally Ian Bowater had to leave in order to be home by Christmas, whereas I, with no family commitments, was able to stay on. The result was that I came away from Melbourne with a valuable contract as well as a lasting friendship. When Sir Keith later came over to help Winston Churchill organise the information side of the War effort he came to our cottage in Oxfordshire for a weekend. (This was in November 1941.)

I was back in England by January 1933, having stopped over at Cairo to see the Pyramids, and at Zermatt, to sample the skiing. With the help of the Orient Express, I was in London before the *S.S. Orford* docked, at the end of the voyage from Australia. I had been round the world under the most comfortable circumstances and with ample leisure, at the company's expense. What a contrast with my life in New York!

CHAPTER XII

Friendships

I was in New York for the 1933 Easter Parade, immortalised in the ditty: 'In your Easter bonnet, with all the flowers upon it, you'll be the finest lady in the Easter Parade.' Walking up Fifth Avenue with the traditional gardenia in my buttonhole I met a fellow Welshman named Gareth Jones and we stopped to talk. Gareth told me he was living with a Russian family in New York in order to learn enough Russian to go to Georgia where there was rumoured to be a terrible famine. Gareth was employed by the London *Daily Telegraph* as a special correspondent, and he told me his highest ambition was to have his name on a newspaper bill board. Later on, in Manchuria, Gareth was to discover an unknown war – the Japanese invasion of Manchuria. For several days the *Telegraph* printed Gareth's despatches. Then a week of silence, until coming out of the Reform Club, I caught sight of a bill board on the pavement outside the Athenæum which read: 'Gareth Jones Murdered.' At the cost of his life Gareth had fulfilled his ambition.

Through Gareth I met Ifor Lloyd, and the two proposed me for membership of the Reform Club. Although only 25, I was elected and have been a member ever since. Ifor had been at Winchester with Charles Bosanquet, and introduced me to him. We struck up an immediate friendship which had the most important consequences for it led to my marrying Charles' sister Rosemary in 1937. In 1933 Charles was managing the Friends Provident Insurance Company. He went on to become Treasurer of Christ Church and the first Vice-Chancellor of the University of Newcastle. To all our family Charles has been the soul of generosity, hospitality, and steady and unshakeable moral support. As a family we owe him an eternal 'thank you'. I will return to our marriage, but that is still four years away. In all this the hand of Providence could be seen. Had I not emigrated to the U.S.A. I should not have met Gareth Jones, who was to be the vital link in the creation of our family.

In the midst of celebrating Christmas 1934 with my parents I received a telephone call from Doane in New York. My salary was to be increased to $8,000 a year and I was instructed to open an English office as quickly as possible. An accountant was on his way to help set up the office and I was to be the managing director. We incorporated British International Paper Limited on 10 January, 1935, and I was its chairman and managing director for the next 38 years. The business flourished. We now had a tenth of the market including important contracts with Beaverbrook Newspapers, the *News Chronicle* and the *Manchester Guardian*. My solicitor, who sat on the Board, was Thomas (later Sir Thomas) Overy. He and his partner Allen were Edward VIII's solicitors in the Abdication Crisis. Thomas Overy was the perfect solicitor, helpful, adroit, clear minded, quick, humorous. My accountant Matt Tennant was another inspired choice: we became firm friends and stood Godfather to each others' children and stayed together for the whole of our business careers. I was singularly fortunate in my colleagues. Now, at 27, I had virtually my own business, which had grown steadily and was to go on growing. With employers 3,000 miles away and no aeroplanes I had considerable liberty from day to day. My principals in New York were not too concerned about what I did: what mattered to them were the results.

Increasingly I felt my home was in England because that was where my friends were. Michael Huxley, Charles Bosanquet, Ifor Lloyd, Rex Stanley (my closest friend at LSE who later left the London Underground Railway to be a sheep farmer in Australia) were all close friends and I had an equally delightful group of women friends. Michael introduced me to his sister Anne and through her to a wide circle of Huxley friends in and about Oxford. Weekends were spent walking, laughing and making music. We would start and finish at the Huxley home on Boars Hill. I still see in imagination the Alfred Munnings watercolour

43

of a rider on horseback surrounded by gorse bushes, over the mantlepiece at Boars Hill, although I had no thought then of collecting. However, in February 1935 I did buy a book from Lionel Robinson, whose bookshop was opposite the Reform Club. It was a first folio of Montaigne's *Essays* 1603, in original binding and cost me £140, £40 of which was to be on credit. My father was not amused. He thought, and said, that I had been smitten by book madness. Little did he, or I for that matter, know how much fine books and pictures were to influence my life.

CHAPTER XIII

Work & Marriage

My work was not only interesting but at times dramatic. In 1932 Price Brothers, one of Canada's leading newsprint producers, was heading for bankruptcy. The industry, of which International Paper was the largest single producer, was operating at between 70% and 60% of capacity, and the difference between these two figures could mean survival or ruin. In an effort to stabilise the price of newsprint, the leader of the British industry, Eric Bowater (later Sir Eric) decided to bid for Price Brothers and thus secure a leading position in Canada as well as in England. International did not want Bowater to obtain a foothold in Canada. The stage was set for a dramatic conflict.

In November I received a cable instructing me to catch the *Aquitania* bound from Southampton to New York and to travel incognito. Eric Bowater was also on board travelling incognito (i.e. not on the passenger list). I knew him by sight but we had not then met. On arrival, Eric proceeded to Canada while I spent two weeks discussing the position with my chiefs, Graustein and Doane, and working out a plan. We would make an offer to the Daily Express Group which they could not resist, and thereby take out of the world market, including Price Brothers, the largest block of uncommitted tonnage likely to be used as an instrument with which to 'beat' the price still further. The timing of our offer was crucial. Eric was due to sail back to England on Norddeutscher Lloyd's *Bremen* and the ship was due to leave at 10 p.m. At 9 p.m. I was still in conference with Graustein and Doane, and warned them I should miss the boat unless I left at once. Thereupon Graustein phoned Norddeutscher Lloyd and told them that the departure of the *Bremen* must be delayed for half an hour and he would pay the cost. I got my final instructions, hailed a taxi, and crept on board under Eric Bowater's very nose. He, like other passengers, had no idea why the ship's departure was being delayed. Before the *Bremen* docked at Southampton I telephoned ahead for a car and chauffeur and arranged with the purser to leave the ship an hour before general disembarkation. Before 1 p.m. I had signed a new agreement with the Express Group for 70,000 tons a year for 5 years which nullified Eric Bowater's plan. The official historian of Bowaters wrote: 'The battle for control of Price Brothers was one of the few battles Eric Bowater lost.'*

Things were going well; too well, and I was due for a setback. When it came, it was self-inflicted. While on a walking holiday in Austria in June 1936 I persuaded a charming young English woman to marry me. She was a friend of my friends and at first it all seemed right, although I had to make my proposal in the presence of a third party who considered it her duty to chaperone us. I was accepted, but on reaching home we found her parents had gone into opposition. This led to a conflict of loyalties which ended in my young lady jilting me after the date of the wedding was fixed and presents were arriving. It was a rude shock.

Then something like a miracle occurred. Charles Bosanquet invited me to spend Christmas with him at the family home at Rock, Northumberland. As soon as I set eyes on Charles' sister Roma, who was 18 and in her first year as a scholar at Somerville, I felt my heart leap for joy. I experienced a total and wonderful assurance that all was to be well. And so it has proved. Before I left Rock we both knew we had met our life's partner.

I was anxious to get married, as already war loomed on the horizon and we should be caught up in it. Roma very gallantly and unselfishly agreed to leave Oxford after one year, and we would marry in September (1937). But then something happened which could have ended the story. In February I was skiing at Lech in Austria with a large party of friends which included Sir Clifford and Lady Norton, Algernon Blackwood, and a doctor by the name of Nesfield who had been barred from practising by the General Medical Council because of an article he had written for

*Bowater, a History, CUP, 1981, p.107

46

the *Daily Express* on the health value of the wheat germ. In July I again found myself in the midst of important negotiations, involving many millions of pounds, with the Daily Express Group. We were almost in agreement when I fell ill. I was alone in my parents' house at Walton-on-Thames as they had gone for a holiday in South Africa.

I dragged myself up to the City to see Thomas Overy, who gave me a glass of brandy to drink, the worst thing I could have taken as it turned out.

At midday I telephoned Dr Nesfield. His secretary said the doctor was too busy to see me. But as I persisted she relented and eventually told me to come in the lunch hour. I showed the doctor a poisoned finger but he was not interested. He had me lie down on a couch and felt my stomach. Then he telephoned his friend, the senior surgeon at Charing Cross Hospital, who came at once and operated for acute peritonitis. I had been within an hour or two of death, I was told. In coming to the assistance of Dr Nesfield the surgeon also risked being barred. I owed him my life. We signed the newsprint contracts a few days later, using my hospital bed as a table. One consequence was that our marriage had to be postponed. When Roma came to see me in the nursing home I could feel nothing and was unsure of everything, and virtually broke off our engagement. This was hard on Roma as she had left Oxford and was busy preparing our cottage for occupation after our wedding. But being of Huguenot and Quaker stock she kept calm and by September we were on track again. The postponement of our wedding gave Roma six weeks to wait which she filled with voluntary work in West Cumberland, then one of the depressed areas where unemployment was greatest.

We had a warm sunny day for our marriage in Rock Church on 5 November. After a train journey and a first night in London at the Berkeley Hotel, we drove in our open Renault two seater to Newhaven. The bill for bed and breakfast at the Berkeley was £2.15s.od. and I still have the receipt. When I showed it to the manager of the new Berkeley Hotel (in 1989) he remarked that the bill today would be one hundred times as much.

The secret of a happy marriage was revealed to me in the next two nights. On the ship to Dieppe we had separate bunks, an upper and a lower. I was tired and made a remark which showed it. There was no reply. Next night Roma was tired, and made a remark which I thought unnecessary. I copied her and kept silence. The secret revealed then, and ever after, is 'never reply to impatience – keep silence.' We have been practising the art ever since and it has yet to fail us.

We were very happy in our thatched cottage at Kidmore End, seven miles north of Reading. We were on glebeland, opposite the Church and there was an orchard as well as a garden. The cottage is listed and illustrated in Batsford's book *The English Cottage* and Cromwell is reputed to have stabled his horses there, which accounts for the name 'Cromwell Cottage'. There can't have been many horses, for there was only one big living room with a huge hearth and three small bedrooms above. The best bedroom was in the modern annexe, and underneath it a formal room not much used except for the Steinway grand. I had bought this piano in 1936 after spending a month playing on every 6 foot piano in Steinway's George Street showrooms until I had found the one with – for me – the perfect tone. The tonal differences that occur between supposedly identical pianos are remarkable.

I have twice mentioned having had the blessing of spiritual guidance at critical moments, at prep. school and when looking for work in the Great Depression. A third such moment occurred during the time of my engagement to Roma. I was walking and thinking about our forthcoming marriage when suddenly I felt myself transported into another world. There it was given me to see that marriage is in itself perfect and the only perfect institution known to men. I saw that the institution of marriage is self-correcting, self-healing and self-balancing, if only we give it a chance to work. There is of course a condition: fidelity. This certainty, and its accompanying beauty, is not something I can describe, but its effect has never left me, so powerful, so beautiful, it was and is.

CHAPTER XIV

The *Geographical Magazine* & other Enthusiasms

I have been blessed in my friends. Michael Huxley has already been mentioned. We met coming home on the *Mauritania* in April 1932. The weather was warm and Michael and Ottilie and their two children, Tom and Selma, sat on the boat deck while I played peasant tunes on my Swiss accordion (I had learnt to play this instrument in 1924 when living with a French speaking family at Neuchâtel). Michael was returning to England to resign his position and prospects in the Foreign Office in favour of starting a new periodical to be called the *Geographical Magazine*. Most people would have been content to aim high editorially while making sure of the magazine's commercial success. Not Michael. He was a perfectionist from the outset, and saw the magazine as an educational adventure with a social purpose. Accordingly half the profits of the magazine were to be channelled into a trust for the promotion of geographical knowledge and research, administered by the Royal Geographical Society.

Michael had a fine mind, no whit inferior to that of Aldous and Julian his famous cousins. He was a born teacher with the quality that makes the teacher outstanding: limitless enthusiasm for the good and true, accompanied by withering hostility to the second rate. Michael's geographical interests were world-wide, and included Halford Mackinder's geo-politic, the Byzantine Empire before 1495, and respect for Nature and its finiteness. In his concern for the environment Michael was well ahead of his time.

I became a director of the *Geographical Magazine* in 1935 and Chairman in 1956, when the magazine was sold to *The Times* as a result of the publishers deciding to pull out. In the course of time the magazine passed to Odhams, but half the profits continue to go in trust to the Royal Geographical Society.

It was Michael who encouraged me to write my first book *The Future of Private Enterprise* which received wide publicity and was published in several countries, as we shall see. Michael and I shared a common belief in virtue as the bond of a democratic society. John Milton had said that virtue 'is the only genuine source of political and individual liberty', a truth echoed a century later by Montesquieu in *The Spirit of the Laws*. My concern was to promote the creation of responsible economic institutions able to contain and canalise the cooperative instincts of ordinary men and women in the workplace.

The *Geographical Magazine* was not my only outside interest in the two years between our marriage and the second World War. I continued visiting Lambeth, where Alford House was flourishing as a men's and boys' club. There in the Lambeth Walk one became conscious of the great weight of unnecessary unhappiness created by unemployment. Something must be done about it. I spoke to my friends and we agreed to form an action group. Michael Huxley, Charles Bosanquet, Clem Leslie and I were its original members. Leslie was a Rhodes scholar and philosopher. Charles was running the Friends Provident Insurance Co. We each agreed to produce papers (they lie before me as I write). Our starting point was that the rate of unemployment was intolerable, averaging 14% between 1921 and 1936. The mind of the group was to do something to encourage the start-up of small businesses and workshops on existing factory sites where light, heat and power would be readily available. We got in touch with Herbert Morrison, then secretary of the London Labour Party, who agreed to meet us, bringing some of his colleagues including Walter (afterwards Lord) Citrine. We worked through 1936 and 1937 and on 4 October 1938 I wrote a letter to *The Times* on behalf of the group outlining a strategy for dealing with unemployment based on the encouragement of schemes of self-help and 'experiments in communal food production for the older unemployed'. The youngest unemployed were to be given the means and tools for rebuilding their community. We thought the return of industry to the Special Areas must wait upon the workers. What we envisaged was a series of regionalised, statutory corporations with the power of initiating and establishing undertakings primarily for the benefit of the unemployed – starting with food production and rehousing, with the cooperation of local authorities.

Our proposals went to the Special Areas Commissioner, whose predecessor Sir Malcolm Stewart had urgently recommended the application of unorthodox methods to find a solution to the unemployment problem.

All these plans were to be overtaken in the run-up to the Second World War in 1939.

During the winters of 1935 and 1936 I went to Austria to ski and as a result made two new friends, both Austrian – Hans Falkner was a guide at Obergurgl. We skied, and in the summer climbed together, I being the novice and Hans the expert. When Hitler invaded Austria, Hans fled by night to the West. His colleague was shot and killed by the Nazis in the act of ski-ing over the border. Hans escaped and came to England where I arranged for him to sail to Canada on one of our newsprint ships. Hans went west and opened up new ski-ing areas of which I believe Aspen, Colorado was one. After the war Hans was able to return to Obergurgl and resume his life there.

Another ski-ing friend was Felix Weiss. He had already made his reputation in Vienna as a monumental sculptor, but was unknown abroad. Like Falkner, Felix had to leave Austria on account of the Nazis as he was part Jewish. I think it was in the King's Road, Fulham, that Felix set up his London studio where he soon became fashionable and sculpted the Earl of Plymouth, David Lloyd George, Lady Eden, the Duke of Windsor, King George VI and many other celebrities. But the threat of war made Felix insecure and he asked me to help him get to America, so we put him on another of our newsprint ships armed with letters of introduction. In his first letter from Canada Felix said he was working on the bust of the Canadian Prime Minister Mackenzie King.

While still in London, and carried away by enthusiasm, Felix had bought a huge 12 cylinder Daimler identical to that used by George VI. One day he told me he was only getting 8 m.p.g., so we took the car to the Daimler service station in the Edgware Road, only to be told that there would be a deposit of £100 to pay before they would lift the bonnet. So Felix sold his car.

In the U.S.A. Felix made rapid progress. He was paid a million dollars for one sculpture, the Washington Memorial to the storming of Iwo Jima by the Marines which stands 85 feet high facing the Lincoln Memorial and the White House. It took Felix nine years to complete. In Washington D.C. Felix has 25 public monuments, none of them to me more impressive than the lovely terracotta bust Felix did of Rosemary and gave us as a wedding present. It was exhibited on a plinth at our pre-wedding party at Crosby Hall on 1 November 1937. In accepting our invitation Felix wrote (on the 7 October):

'I am so happy that you like the bust I did of Rosemary and I hope it portrays her beauty and describes her beautiful person-ality and character only a little bit, because she is so lovely and has so many fine qualities to make you very happy, which I wish from the depth of my heart. I am working here in Venice on the bust of HRH the Princess Alexandra of Greece and shall return to London next week and am looking forward to see you and meanwhile sending my very kindest regards.

Ever yours, Felix'

This is a fair example of Felix's sensitive command of English. Another comes from the speech Felix made at the unveiling of his Memorial to the American Red Cross in Washington D.C. on 25 June 1959:

'I have tried to show those people giving generously of them-selves to alleviate suffering, always ready to serve with strong arms and with warmth and sympathy. Next to love, sympathy is the divinest passion of the human heart. He who bestows compassion communicates his own soul.'

When Felix married he changed his name to Felix Weiss de Weldon.

Another visitor was Jim Forrester otherwise Lord Verulam.

He often stayed with us while putting together his Association for Planning and Regional Reconstruction, arguably the first planning body in England. Jim was a severe critic. He told Rosemary all our saucepans were of the wrong shape.

One cannot always choose one's friends, but the friendship of books is within one's own discretion, and when one wants them they are at hand, not in Washington or Obergurgl. Now that I was settled in England (1935) I began seriously to collect books and to read them, preferably in the original edition. Consciously or unconsciously I was making up for not being allowed to go to Oxford or Cambridge. By 1938 I had over 600 volumes. The first item in the Inventory of September 1938 is Baskerville's great Bible of 1761 in contemporary red morocco, a collector's book if there ever was one, as it was almost too large to fit into our thatched cottage. Amongst other rarities I bought were:

> Hobbes' *Leviathan* 1651
> Spenser's *Faerie Queen* 1611
> St Augustine's *City of God* 1610
> Sir Thomas More's *Works* 1557
> W. Tindale's *New Testament* 1536
> John Donne's *Sermons* 3 vols 1640, 1649, 1661
> Keats *Lamia* 1820, uncut
> White's *Selborne* 1789
> and thirty or more William Pickerings.

I had not met Geoffrey Keynes, but was already using his bibliographies, especially those of W. Pickering and W. Blake. Whatever I collected had to be in good condition and in a contemporary binding. I disliked imperfect books and found support from the trade, especially from Ernest, Kenneth and Bryan Maggs to whose friendship and support I owe so much during three successive generations of Maggs Brothers.

I had also begun to collect Blake, starting with a proof set of the Job *Engravings* (1825).

None of these books cost £100. The Baskerville *Prayer Book*, the most beautiful book of its kind, cost less than a twentieth of this. I already had six of these and was later able to give one to each of our eight children, a strong argument for starting to collect early. My wife and I have used the Baskerville *Prayer Book* for our private devotions ever since.

Our first child, Dan, was born on 26 August 1938 and completed our domestic happiness. It was a time of deep content, although the shadow of Munich and the threat of Hitler hung over us. The Steinway grand piano was being played. I was fortunate enough to find a music teacher, Mrs McKnight Kauffer, the wife of the poster artist, who had studied in Paris under Philippe. She was an inspirational teacher and we became fast friends with her and her family.

CHAPTER XV

The War & Lord Beaverbrook

On 9 April 1940 Hitler invaded Norway and the Baltic was closed. The real world war had begun. Supplies of pulp and paper from Scandinavia were cut off and North America became overnight the sole source of the raw material of the British Press.

On 29 April I was summoned to Lord Beaverbrook's home, Stornoway House, overlooking Green Park, and shown into a large room where Lord Beaverbrook introduced himself with Lord Camrose. They wasted no time on pleasantries but came to the point. The Newspaper Society and the Newspaper Proprietors' Association were in session in a room upstairs and they wanted to know if I would undertake for the duration of the War to implement their agreement with the War Cabinet to procure, import, ration and distribute the newsprint required by the British Press, numbering 1,400 newspapers. I replied that I was willing but they must ask my firm's consent. Lord Beaverbrook thereupon dictated a cable to Mr Cullen, president of International Paper Company, New York. It read as follows:

'This message is sent you on behalf of the newspaper proprietors of Great Britain now in session. Will you lend Mr Goyder to us for duration of War. He will be expected to carry out our agreement with Ministry of Supply for purchase, transport, and distribution of our newsprint requirements from Canada and Newfoundland. We propose if you approve to make up his salary to five thousand pounds yearly. Answer to us Stornoway House St James London.'

That night I spoke with Mr Cullen on the transatlantic telephone. We agreed I would accept the job, but not be paid for it. My ordinary salary, about half of what was proposed, would suffice, and leave me free to be my own man in dealing with the intensely competitive newspaper industry of Great Britain. As things turned out, I would need this degree of freedom in order to remain in control.

In cabling his consent Mr Doane added:
'We think this is a fine tribute to yourself and confirms our own feeling as to the good job you are always doing however we know you will appreciate our position in reference to having anyone pay you part of your salary.'

– a remarkably generous comment to receive from the boss at the critical moment in one's career! But that was Richard Doane's way, and it was why I loved the man.

During the first week I reported daily at 9.30 a.m. to Lord Beaverbrook at Stornoway House. On the first day Max said 'let's go for a walk' and we trotted to and fro in Green Park; Max with his arm in mine while he talked about how we would unload newsprint in London and John Scott would collect his ration for the *Manchester Guardian* from week to week and so on. I remained silent. This went on for some time until suddenly, and violently, Max withdrew his arm and exclaimed (or exploded):

'You don't talk; what's the matter? Am I thinking straight?' I replied 'No Sir, you are not thinking straight.' Then Lord Beaverbrook made a truly astonishing statement: 'From now on, Goyder, I will do anything you tell me.' And he was as good as his word throughout the war, as we shall see.

I had already discussed our task with colleagues and it was clear that we should have to unload our ships wherever Hitler's bombs and submarines allowed and for this to be possible the newspapers would have to adopt standard – that is to say inter-changeable – roll sizes. The only newspaper to resist was *The Times*. I got Max to telephone Major Astor and put it to him, did he want to be the only newspaper not in the scheme. Major Astor replied that *The Times* was precluded on technical grounds from altering its printing machines. I whispered to Beaverbrook 'Tell him we've had a team in *The Times* pressroom and the alterations to the machinery will cost £5,000.' Lord Beaverbrook repeated this to Major Astor and added 'Are you in or out?' and the only possible reply was 'in'. Lord Beaverbrook liked this. As for Major

Astor, after the war he asked me to become General Manager of *The Times*. Perhaps this was one reason.

My strength in standing up to Beaverbrook came from my weakness. I had an uneasy conscience about being reserved from bearing arms for my country, and when I spoke as I did I felt my conscience was freed. From then on Lord Beaverbrook treated me as an equal. I outlined my plans daily at 9.30. We would have a company with 12 directors – including all the Press Lords and each contributing a guarantee of one million pounds. The Board would meet every Friday at 11 a.m. in Reuters boardroom. We would buy ships and borrow them, chartering where necessary. Already we had four of our own, plus two belonging to Associated Newspapers. Bowaters lent their two ships. That gave us a fleet of 8. On the third day I reported to Beaverbrook that I had bought two ships lying in San Francisco harbour that had been handed over as German reparations after the First World War. Beaverbrook's reaction: 'We'll have to make you commander in chief of the British Army!' (note the exclamation mark). Finance was no problem. I rang the manager of Lloyds Bank and asked for a loan of a million pounds. 'On what security,' asked the Manager. 'On the security of the British Press' I replied, and got the money in a two minute telephone call.

Our corporate name was 'The Newsprint Supply Company' with Lord Beaverbrook as chairman. In addition we set up a Rationing Committee with Stanley Bell as its Chairman. He was managing director of the *Daily Mail* and had the admirable habit, when he could not reach an agreement between competing newspapers, of adjourning for ten minutes, and then asked the committee to look at the problem from the other end. The committee's function was to devise and maintain an equitable rationing system. My job was to implement decisions. But sometimes I had to act independently, as when I learned the *Daily Worker* could not get any newsprint from the home mills, who said the credit risk was too great. But I felt sure the real reason was that they were unwilling to supply a communist newspaper. I gave instructions for rolls to be cut into sheets to enable the *Daily*

Worker to continue, and justified this on the ground that we were not censors; censorship was for the Home Secretary. In due course Herbert Morrison closed the *Daily Worker*. I was of course a member of the rationing committee and came to admire its impartiality. Eric Bowater was also a member. When one of our members came hot-foot from Whitehall to say the Germans were landing troops and tanks on the Kent coast I knew instinctively that Eric Bowater was my combat leader! Fortunately the rumour turned out to be false, but it lasted long enough for members to display their varying reactions.

Lord Camrose was, apart from Lord Beaverbrook, the most senior member of the Newspaper Proprietors Association. On 12 March 1942 he wrote an article about the Newsprint Supply Company in his newspaper the *Daily Telegraph* in which he said:
'The Newsprint Supply Company was formed in May 1940. From this date this company has controlled and allocated all newsprint used by the newspapers of the country, both home made and imported. The scheme has worked admirably... the plan has been a brilliant success, and it can be safely said that this joint effort has been responsible for the fact that the newspaper Press of the country has been maintained intact... All newspapers large and small have been able to secure their newsprint on exactly the same basis. Not one has had to suspend publication for lack of its raw material – newsprint.'

In his account of the Newsprint Supply Company my assistant, Norman Bezzant, writes 'I do not remember any occasion of your authority being challenged or usurped by board members'. There were however at least two such occasions. The first was in June 1940. Three members of the War Cabinet had been nominated to oversee the work of the company. They were Sir Kingsley Wood (Chancellor), Oliver Lyttelton (Minister of Production) and Brendan Bracken (Minister of Information). I discovered that E. J. Robertson, Managing Director of the *Express*, and Bell of the *Mail*, had set up a meeting with these Ministers to discuss newsprint rationing without telling me. I appealed to Beaverbrook, and threatened to resign. Max said 'Don't. Just go to the meeting as if nothing had happened.' I did so, and sat silently through the meeting. It was the last of its kind to be held!

Our relations with Sir William Palmer at the Ministry of Supply had in any case become so close as to make any further meetings of this particular War Cabinet committee superfluous.

There was one further attempt by Bell and Robertson to take control of the Company. The supervision exercised over individual newspapers in competition with each other had to be absolute. This was achieved by requiring a return of consumption and stock each week. If we thought a newspaper was sending in false returns we sent someone to get the facts and we reported to the rationing committee, who decided in the case of one large provincial newspaper to cut its allocation by one half until its total over-use had been made up. Naturally this created strains and pressures between individual newspapers, when, for example, we forbade the continuance of free gift schemes on the grounds that they used up irreplaceable stocks of paper. I cannot recall the exact reason, but it came to the point that I felt bound to assert my full authority over these and similar *contretemps*, or resign. I telephoned Lord Beaverbrook early on Friday 23 October 1942 and arranged to go down to Cherkely, Beaverbrook's home, the same day. Lord Beaverbrook had resigned from the War Cabinet that February, and was resting from 21 months of feverish activity as Minister of Aircraft Production and as a member of the inner War Cabinet of five. It had been, in Beaverbrook's own words 'twenty one months of high adventure the like of which has never been known before'. But now, in October, he was rested and tranquil, having had his 'period of withdrawal'. The war news was better too. General Montgomery had won the Battle of El Alemain and victory was 'in the air'.

I visited Beaverbrook that afternoon and quote from my notes, written the same day:

'Today to Cherkely to see Beaverbrook. He greets me with the old look of quiet, friendly recognition. "Sit down and tell me what's wrong". I go straight into my story of difficulty in managing Robertson and Bell, talk of denouncing Bell at next board meeting, alternatively of resigning. "What does Robertson say?" So Max gets R. and talks across the phone simultaneously. "Goyder's with me, what's the matter? – Its no good Goyder; Robertson won't do anything to help you. I can't help you, I'm out, I'm not interested anymore in newspapers – that's Robertson's job, not in money or newsprint – I can't help you." We change the subject and then I come back. I ask Beaverbrook to come to next Friday's board as a guest. "Guest? Aren't I chairman of the company?" "Thank you Sir for that." Max livens up. "You talk of resigning. Don't do it. Why not fight? You are the manager of the company. Bell's chairman of the rationing committee. Then go right ahead. Ignore him. Take no notice of him at all. He'll soon be coming to you to know what's going on. Never resign – it's better to be sacked. Let them criticise, let them storm, they can't sack you. So go ahead."

I thank Max for his good advice. He shouts "get me Robertson again. What, another board meeting? he's always at meetings. Get him. That you, Robertson? I've told Goyder to go ahead and see everyone he wants to see. He's the manager and I've told him to manage. That's all right with you? You think he'll tell Bell? No sir, I won't. Goyder says he won't. Goodbye to you."

We walk towards the front hall. Silent. I notice the mantle-piece stripped of family photos. Only one remains, and it is of Stalin, given by him to Beaverbrook. I ask Max a question:

"You were impressed by Stalin?" Max nods. "Do you think we shall have a system like that in England after the war?" No reply. Then he closes his fist and brings it down on the nearby table with a loud bang, saying "I'm an individualist." He repeats these words for a second and third time with increasing emphasis ending almost in a shout. Here is another side to this many-sided man. He loves power and he has seen in Stalin power beyond his dreams. But the exercise of such power is incompatible with the liberty of others, hence the frustration.

We arrive at the front door and Max asks: "How are you going to get back to London?" "By train," I reply. Max says "follow me" and stalks out to the garage, points to an Austin Ten, asks the surprised garage hand if it is useable and says "get in". He drives me to Leatherhead station, drops me on the wrong side of the tracks, says "Goodbye to you" and is gone, leaving me to clamber over the live rails to the station. Obviously Max had not driven there before. Was he paying me a compliment or trying to kill me?

In the official biography of Beaverbrook, A. J. P. Taylor mentions that Max would accompany Sir Hugh Dowding down two flights of stairs at the Ministry of Aircraft Production and would do this for Dowding and for no one else except Churchill. I had been very privileged that day, as I felt when writing my diary that evening: 'Dear beloved Max – what a Man! What greatness. Much calmer than before, almost serenity, yet still the same alertness. I loved Max two years ago. I love him now, and I shall go out and conquer the press lords and their wiles!'

Lord Beaverbrook duly took the chair at the next board meeting as he had promised. There were no further problems. Nothing was said, but the victory was complete. No ill will came of this. If anything Robertson – Beaverbrook's right hand man – and I became better friends. In 1946 we entertained the entire Robertson family at Henley Regatta. When we negotiated our next contract Robertson started by asking 'How much newsprint do you want to sell us, Goyder?' I replied hopefully, 100,000 tons a year. Robertson answered: 'No, it will be 127,500 tons a year', an amount equal to 10% of the entire newsprint consumption of Britain.

This is not all I owed Lord Beaverbrook. During the first week of May 1940 I was often alone with him as he negotiated to bring about Neville Chamberlain's downfall. To one M.P. after another Beaverbrook spoke on the phone: to Amery, Sam Hoare, Archibald Sinclair. It was Leopold Amery who led the attack on the Prime Minister in the House of Commons with his 'In the name of God, go,' but I heard Beaverbrook put these words to Amery on the telephone beforehand. I also heard Max advise Chamberlain to put the question of confidence to a vote in the House of Commons. On 8 May Beaverbrook wrote to

Chamberlain to the same effect. Chamberlain resigned two days later.

During these negotiations I asked Max: 'What do you hope to get out of all your efforts to change the government' and he replied 'I would like to be offered the Ministry of Agriculture. I have campaigned for British agriculture for years.' Six days later Max became Minister of Aircraft Production, where through his prodigious energy the fighter aircraft needed to win the Battle of Britain were produced and thereby spared us from invasion. This was the beginning of what Beaverbrook himself described as the most glorious era of his life. Churchill called it 'Beaverbrook's hour'.

With Lord Beaverbrook's constant support and encouragement I remained manager of the Newsprint Supply Company until the summer of 1947. When I retired, the following leading article in the *Newspaper World* (24 June 1947) appeared:

'Mr George Goyder is a wholehearted believer in the type of cooperative enterprise symbolised by the Newsprint Supply Company and he has brought to his duties an enthusiasm which enabled him to shoulder the heavy responsibilities of the war years and the post-war period. His efficient control of the activities of the company has contributed much to the smoothness with which the company has operated. He well deserves Lord Rothermere's appreciation of his services to the British Press.'

Lord Rothermere wrote formally and appreciatively. Lord Beaverbrook's letter of (18 June 1947) was more personal:
'Dear Goyder,

I am sorry to hear you are retiring from the management of the Newsprint Supply Company Limited.

I congratulate you warmly on a very fine job during the past seven years. We were fortunate in having your services. You made a big contribution to the Press of Britain when this country was fighting bitterly for world freedom. I wish you all success and thank you for writing to me. Be sure to let me know how you are getting on.

Yours sincerely, Beaverbrook.'

The Press Lords went so far in their thanks as to ask me what I would like by way of return. On the spur of the moment I said 'bibles'. The Harmsworth bible collection was being sold a week hence and I had my eye on some of the books in the sale at Sotheby's. How much do you want? I replied: £5,000. A cheque was made out and Lord Layton gave it to me. A week later I returned half the money. The 1611 King James Bible I so much wanted turned out to be in an ugly Victorian binding. Although the book fetched £2,000 I didn't want it. A few weeks later I found another copy in quarto. It was the genuine 'He' Bible in contemporary calf; it cost me £5 and I still have it. I think there is a moral in this story somewhere, perhaps a case of trusting one's luck rather than one's judgment!

Although I won most of my battles with Robertson and Bell, I was equally guilty of using the Newsprint Supply Company for my own purposes, which is what they were doing. My private purpose was to show that a company can be both efficient and idealistic. When I wrote to Lord Beaverbrook saying I hoped he would agree that 'The cooperative non-profit method of distribution had justified itself' and expressed my hope that after the war it would help cure unemployment, Max replied 'You are not justified in treating the Newsprint Supply Company as a co-operative non-profit movement. It is a manifestation of capitalism and not new at that.' (13 May 1941).

A few months later Lord Camrose in the *Daily Telegraph* referred to the Newsprint Supply Company as 'entirely a cooperative organisation working for the industry as a whole. It was not formed as a profit-making enterprise and the Articles of Association do not provide for any distribution in the way of dividends.'

In other words it was all right for a newspaper baron to admit the Company was designed to serve an unselfish purpose, but not for one of its servants to do so. How fortunate I had been in not accepting a salary! On 22 April, 1941 the *London Star* diarist commented as follows:

'The discussion which has arisen on the basis of the Newsprint

Supply Company provides an interesting example of the flexibility of a war-time organisation. Mr George Goyder, general manager of the Company, has described it as one of the portents of a new social order in which private profit will be eliminated. Lord Camrose in his reply (in *The Times* newspaper) says that this is erroneous: the company has been formed to buy and distribute newsprint for newspapers, who could not exist if they did not make a profit. It is, of course, true that there is no question of profit-making in the actual running of the company, which is an agent for the whole industry. Mr Goyder's contention is idealistic. Mr Goyder himself is an idealist, but he combines sincerity of motive and the utmost probity with a remarkably able, far-seeing mind. I should call him the practical idealist.'

Six years later, when the time came for my resignation, the editor of *World's Press News* wrote a leader saying that my duties had been carried out 'with a fine sense of justice'. However exaggerated these comments, they at least made clear what I was trying to do. I believe absolute justice is beyond mortal man to discover, let alone practise. But still, I believe it is the right goal to seek.

Managing the Newsprint Supply Company was not however, in spite of these pleasant comments, a sinecure. Two examples will suffice.

In one August weekend in 1941 the German Air Force bombed our newsprint stocks simultaneously in London, Liverpool and Glasgow and we lost a quarter of the total national stock. We then took the unprecedented step of dispersing the remaining stock of paper to open storage on farms well away from the cities. This was made possible by the use of tents of corrugated iron, the invention of a member of our staff which was later copied by the Ministry of Food for housing stocks of sugar. Open storage turned out to be very efficient; the damage was only 2% compared with 1% under normal warehouse conditions.

Our losses at sea were worse: eight out of our twelve ships were torpedoed with heavy loss of life. One ship was sunk off the coast of Newfoundland on Christmas Eve in a Force 8 gale. Two of the crew rowed back to St John's only to be burned to death in a fire in the Sailors' Hostel on Christmas day. Another seaman scrambled onto an invasion raft, where he endured four weeks of Atlantic weather before being picked up off the north east of Scotland by a Polish destroyer. He had drifted with the Gulf Stream right across the Atlantic Ocean and appeared to be none the worse for his ordeal. He told me he owed his life to finding two objects in a pocket of his raft: a tin of grease and a cabbage. While this was going on his wife was bombed out of their house in South London. When she came to tell me this, she affirmed her conviction that her husband was alive and she would see him again. This story made the front page of the *Daily Mirror*.

CHAPTER XVI

Youth Service Volunteers

I still kept in touch with Alford House in the Lambeth Walk. The Old Millhillians were firmly in control, but our usual volunteers were away on active war service and we had to bring in a professional social worker, F. A. Bracey, to run the club. Together we conceived the idea of running summer camps for youth where labour was urgently required to pick fruit, fell timber and harvest. To avoid any suggestion of conscription we called the organisation Youth Service Volunteers and asked five eminent people to act as Trustees: Sir Wyndham Deedes, Sir Malcolm Stewart, Sir Richard Livingstone, Sam Courtauld and Sir Walter Citrine of the T.U.C., all of whom accepted.

In addition to Sam Courtauld, two other friends joined the board who were Basil (afterwards Sir Basil) Smallpeice and Lord Verulam. YSV received a good deal of newspaper publicity. *The Times Educational Supplement* for 11 December 1943 had this to say about us:

'The organisation seeks to achieve a complete mixing of all social classes and all varieties of occupation and first hand investigation has revealed how successfully this has been achieved. *Thus the great tradition of the Duke of York's Camps is being continued*' (my italics)

In our first full season we were overwhelmed by the number of applications – over 30,000. Our twenty one camps could accommodate only a fraction of those asking to come. We had hit upon an idea that appealed to the young. But with supervisory staff practically unobtainable we were forced to limit our operations. Both Sir Malcolm Stewart and Sam Courtauld backed us to the hilt financially so that we did not need to ask for state funds. Nevertheless the truth is that we suffered from being too successful, illustrating my father's maxim that more businesses fail through too rapid growth than from any other reason. After the war Youth Service Volunteers continued under the shortened name Concordia. It was, I believe the first youth service organisation of its kind in Britain.

CHAPTER XVII

The Times

One June day in the summer of 1947 Major Astor, who was both the proprietor of *The Times* and a director of the Newsprint Supply Company, asked me to meet him at the Athenæum, and in the course of lunch offered me the management of *The Times*. He told me that my control of *The Times* would be shared with the editor, subject only to the Board of Directors. I asked Major Astor if he would tell me why I had been chosen for such a distinguished position, and in what way he was dissatisfied with *The Times*? The reply was that this was not the reason I was being asked. I said I would like the weekend to consider the matter and to talk it over with my wife. She was attracted by the prestige the job carried, not for its own sake but for the good one could do from such a position. I was against the idea. If it had been like the Newsprint Supply Company, a case of innovation, I might have taken the job for a few years. But the idea of devoting the rest of my business life to *The Times* did not appeal to me. It was not what I had gone into business for. My pledge and my calling was to try to find out what was wrong with industry and do something to put it right. In retrospect I see another, and more practical reason for declining to join the Fleet Street fraternity. None of my friends who then managed national newspapers lived long. The only one I know of who is alive as I write is John Dawson of the *Express* and he got out early.

Nor was I much attracted by a parallel offer from Geoffrey (later Lord) Crowther to become manager of the *News Chronicle*. Reconciling the views of the proprietor and managing director of that newspaper would be, and soon showed itself to be, an impossible task. The *News Chronicle* was doomed. It did not have the unifying policy of its proprietor as had the *Daily Express*.

There was also family life to think of. By now we had five children, and had moved to a lovely old rectory near Henley-on-Thames which we called Pindars.

CHAPTER XVIII

The Laity Challenge Fund

I was looking for a different challenge, and it came in the form of a meeting called by the Bishop of Oxford in 1948 to consider the financial plight of the Oxford Diocesan clergy, whose average income was £320 a year, lower than that of any other English diocese with the exception of Ripon. I agreed to become the first Hon. Treasurer of what we called the Laity Challenge Fund. Without realising it, we were setting up the first Anglican Stewardship movement in England. Lord Hambleden became our chairman and Pat Hamilton our secretary and between the three of us we visited most of the 600 parishes in the diocese and earned ourselves mental and physical, but fortunately only temporary, breakdowns. We found poverty, apathy, and something like despair among the parochial clergy, with their wives chained to the sink and lacking the means to live a sociable existence, unless they or their spouses were lucky enough to have had a private income. In most parishes the laity were apathetic. It was to be a long haul before the idea of stewardship was taken up by the Central Board of Finance.

The immediate effect of speaking at dozens of parish meetings was to quicken my interest in the church generally, and in the Church of England in particular. I had found what I had been seeking in the way of a second career. As a result of taking on the task of stewardship (which in practice means loving and caring for the clergy as part of one's Christian duty and witness) I was elected within eighteen months as a member of the Church Assembly representing the Oxford Diocese, and continued to be a member of this body and its successor, the National Synod, until 1975. I shall return to this subject in Chapter XXIV.

CHAPTER XIX

The Future of Private Enterprise

In 1940 I had been introduced by Sir Frederick Ogilvie of the BBC to Joe (J. H.) Oldham, today widely regarded as the founder of the ecumenical movement. Joe was actively engaged in setting up two lay Christian bodies, to be known respectively as 'The Moot' and 'The Christian Frontier Council'. The Moot was to be a group of philosophers which included T. S. Eliot, Alec Vidler, Dr Demant, Professor Hodges and Philip Mairet. I attended a meeting at which T. S. Eliot spoke of his vision of a Christian Community as distinct from a community of Christians. Middleton Murry was there. He had published a book in 1933 on William Blake in which he sought to explain Blake's 'fourfold vision'. I invited him down for the weekend to Cromwell Cottage and he came and seemed to enjoy himself talking about Blake.

But the Christian Frontier Council was more in my line. It consisted of some 30 Christian laymen who were thought by their contemporaries and by Dr Oldham to be 'coming' men and women and who already had serious public responsibilities. We met monthly and published a weekly journal, *The Christian Newsletter*, which was edited by Joe and contained articles contributed by the members, who included several men and women destined to make their mark: John (afterwards Lord) Redcliffe-Maud, Henry Brooke, who became Home Secretary and a life peer, (Dame) Barbara Ward, Basil (afterwards Sir Basil) Smallpeice, Sam Courtauld, Sir Wilfred Garrett and Sir Basil Blackwell.

Among our contributors was the then Archbishop of York, William Temple. He wrote an article for *The Christian Newsletter* entitled 'Begin Now' in which he called for a social revolution after the War to bring the worker into partnership with the employer. The article came out in August 1940, when the Battle of

Britain was at its height and a German invasion appeared imminent. A few short quotations will give the 'feel' of William Temple's thinking:

'The profit motive has become the dominant motive. It is this which has led to the sacrilegious sacrifice of rural England ... It has turned man into an economic animal ... If we are to dethrone the profit motive from its predominance how is this to be done? ... Begin now ... In return for limited liability, insist upon the limitation of profits and dividends. Apply the principle of the Mosaic Law known as the Jubilee. Give labour access to the board of directors as of right.'

This was, and is, radical stuff. Temple made it clear that he was out to 'reverse the reversal of the natural order' in which consumption had been made subject to production and production subject to finance, whereas the natural order places consumption first and finance last. Temple went on, as Archbishop of York, to elaborate (but not to change) his views, in his book *Christianity and Social Order*, which Penguin issued in 1942. It is a passionate plea for a new social order based on justice.

As a young man Temple had been to Jena for a conference on philosophy, and while there (1905) he met some of the leaders in the Carl Zeiss optical glass organisation. In *Christianity and Social Order* Temple mentions Zeiss as an example of a company run as a trust on behalf of the workers, community and University of Jena. The Webbs had already in 1914 described Zeiss as 'the most elaborately perfected industrial organisation that the world has ever seen'.

I had begun writing *The Future of Private Enterprise* and in order to illustrate my thesis of the social responsibility of the company I was eager to find examples of companies which were successful, while being run for the common benefit, including that of the employees. In USA the great firm of Sears Roebuck provided a shining example. In Britain there was, and is, the John Lewis Partnership. But the example that seemed to stand out above all others was the Carl Zeiss Stiftung or Foundation. How was I to get the facts?

In January 1946 I sent a nine page memorandum on responsibility in the economic system (written for discussion in the Christian Frontier Council) to Sir Stafford Cripps, then President of the Board of Trade. Towards the end of this rather long document I mentioned Zeiss. Sir Stafford replied in his own hand asking: 'Could you let me have the full details of the Jena arrangement as although I have heard about this I do not know where to get a copy in this country.'

I made inquiries and learned that the War Office had translated the Zeiss constitution into English and I sent a copy to Sir Stafford. At the same time Rosemary and I resolved to visit Oberkochen in West Germany where Zeiss had settled after escaping from Jena, now in the Russian Zone. The account I wrote after visiting Oberkochen in 1950 is quoted at length by Robert Oakeshott in his study *The Carl Zeiss Stiftung; its first hundred years of Trust ownership* published in 1990 by Partnership Research Limited with help from the Anglo-German Foundation.

With the permission of the Zeiss directors I published an English version of the Zeiss Statute in *The Future of Private Enterprise* (1951) and in its sequel *The Responsible Company* (1961).

In retrospect I believe it was the influence of William Temple that decided me to set out in quest of the responsible company, just as it was Temple's influence which encouraged me to go all out (once I had been elected to the Church Assembly) for synodical government, and so to fulfil the main aim of the Life and Liberty Movement which Temple and Dick Sheppard had begun in 1917.

Bernard Shaw somewhere remarks that it takes sixty years to bring about a constitutional revolution in Britain. Between 1951 and 1963 I made a number of speeches in the Church Assembly which led in 1970 to the introduction of Synodical Government. I had no inkling in 1951 that I was starting a reform of the Church of England which was to be described in the official handout for the special service in Westminster Abbey on 4 November 1970 (inaugurating the National Synod), as 'a constitutional association of great historic importance' and 'a new era in the government of the Church'. It had taken fifty-three years (from 1917 to 1970) to bring about synodical government. Industrial reform has proved an even harder nut to crack. I am convinced that the public limited liability company has to be redesigned in accordance with the natural law, which among other things prohibits usury, but then one has to establish the practicalities of the responsible company. This is what gave such importance to the Zeiss constitution with its established record of success since 1905. But as I write (September 1992) we are still some way from legislating for the responsible company, although an increasing number of companies are becoming concerned with their social responsibilities.

During 1942-44 Sam Courtauld, Barbara Ward, Basil Smallpeice, Christopher Simmonds and I met monthly as an informal industrial sub-committee of the Christian Frontier Council. We dined as guests of Sam Courtauld at North Audley Street. Two books were hatched by these discussions, Sam Courtauld's collection of addresses under the heading of *Ideals and Industry* published in 1949 by Cambridge University Press, and my book *The Future of Private Enterprise* published in 1951.

In his book Samuel Courtauld argues as a captain of industry that labour is entitled to a seat on the board of directors of the public limited liability company. He is in favour of labour being admitted to share in the highest executive functions of management, and allowed to acquire full knowledge of the financial structure and the policy of the business. He is wholehearted in saying 'I advocate the appointment of labour representatives to the boards of companies'.

Sam Courtauld spent two weekends with us at Cromwell Cottage, in 1943 and 1944. He was the only guest we ever had who insisted on drying the inside surfaces of our forks as carefully as the outside. I remember the glee with which Sam climbed a thirty foot ladder to pick cherries in our orchard, calling down to us 'my son-in-law wouldn't approve,' referring of course, to R. A. Butler. Sam was immensely generous in financing Youth Service Volunteers and treated me almost as a son. He was my ideal of what an industrial giant should be, and he gave me confidence in exploring the social responsibility of industry and writing about it.

Out of our discussions was born the idea of the responsible company and a prophetic view of the future of private enterprise. In the next chapter we shall see how the idea was received.

CHAPTER XX

The Future of Private Enterprise

(continued)

Basil Blackwell published my first book in February 1951. It attracted a good deal of publicity and the reviews were favourable. The *Economist* wrote 'A new moral order – the thing demonstrably works'. The *Observer* said 'a valuable stimulus, useful ideas for developing new industrial policies'. *The Times* and *Sunday Times* expressed approval. A Third Programme talk, reprinted in the *Listener*, provoked a leading article in the *News Chronicle* saying that the book raised issues of importance to everyone in the country. All the main political parties found something of interest to themselves.

The *Tory Challenge* wrote: 'Much of Mr Goyder's thinking is along the lines of the Conservative Industrial Charter – an admirable basis for discussion.'

The left wing *Tribune* commented: 'It may well prove a British and socialist solution. The whole idea is going to be of immense importance to the Labour Movement.'

The liberal *News Chronicle* commented: 'An example of clear, hard thinking in a field of social analysis in which hard, clear thought is vitally necessary by socialists, liberals and conservatives alike.'

The *Federation of British Industry* wrote: 'an able contribution on a vital contemporary theme.'

The Church Press was enthusiastic. *Theology* said: 'Performs a valuable function in analysing the form of the company.'

The Society for Promoting Christian Knowledge wrote: 'It is this intimate knowledge of what it is like inside a firm, coupled with a clear Christian faith and undoubted courage that makes this book worthy of careful study. The attention it has already received in industrial circles is a clear indication that Mr Goyder has his finger on the real issues.'

The one exception was the *Financial Times*. The City of London was hostile and Harold Wincott was employed to demolish my argument. He began his review in these words:

'Whatever else you may call it, you can't dismiss Mr Goyder's book as the embittered attack of an anti-capitalist.'

There was considerable interest on the part of the periodicals.

The *Statist* said: 'Mr Goyder is one of the few non-socialists who appears to have done some really deep thinking about what sort of measures might effectively lead to the classless free-enterprise society.'

The *British Weekly* commented: 'He states his thesis with great clarity and conciseness and an inescapable sense of urgency. The result is a book that no one concerned about human problems of industry can afford to miss.'

There was also radio publicity. I gave a radio talk on 1 May 1952 on the BBC's Third Programme under the heading 'To whom is industry responsible'. Next day the *News Chronicle* referred to my book in its leading article as follows:

'It is a pity that Mr George Goyder's radio talk last night was confined to the Third Programme. He was dealing with a topic that, directly or indirectly, affects everyone in the country – the responsibilities of industry in the community. And he was dealing with it in fresh terms that are bound to arouse controversy.'

Other opportunities for stating the case and for pointing to the solutions proposed in *The Future of Private Enterprise* came in the form of panel discussions on radio. In December 1951 I was the guest of the Fifty One Club where *The Future of Private Enterprise* was debated. One comment I remember was to the effect that to reduce the responsibilities of industry to writing was not an end in itself, but a means of making the end clear. This reminded me of Fritz Schumacher's aphorism:

'Freedom and order – this is the main organisational dilemma – the funny thing is that when you lose one you lose both.' What is true in business is true in theology: there is a Law and a Gospel and both need to be upheld if either is to survive.

Of the many letters I received was one from George Bell, Bishop of Chichester, who wrote: 'I want to tell you how very much I have been impressed by it, and how important it seems to me to be.' Coming from a man of his discernment I found this letter very encouraging.

There was also a reaction from abroad. Italian and Spanish editions were published in 1955 and 1957 respectively and a succession of Japanese translations in 1959, 1963 and 1970. The 1970 Diamond Press edition in Japanese sold 20,000 copies. When *The Responsible Company* came out ten years later (1961) in Japanese, it was to have a fresh translation and a new publisher, Shunjusha.

At home there was a political reaction. My friend Clem Leslie told Herbert Morrison about the book, and Morrison asked to read it in advance of publication (Leslie was Morrison's publicity director). Morrison was at the time (1950) at the peak of his career, being Deputy Prime Minister, Chairman of the Economic Committee of the Party, and Lord President of the Council. There was growing dissatisfaction with the Government's nationalisation policies and complaints were coming in from the unions as well as consumers. A report of the Amalgamated Union of Engineering Workers (AUEW) complained of 'old bosses with new hats, over-centralisation, and top-heavy staffs'. The Government had a majority of only five in the House of Commons after the 1950 election, compared with 146 in 1945. This added to the Government's problems. The general mood was one of dissatisfaction. All this made Herbert Morrison receptive to new ideas.

Having read my book in draft (it came out six months later) Herbert Morrison invited me to lunch to discuss my ideas. A note I made at the time, reads as follows:

'Lunched with Herbert Morrison on 23 October. Mr Morrison in a conversational and friendly mood and extremely informal. He first of all asked me what I was doing and we went on to discuss the newspapers. He said he thought it was a mistake for Pat Bishop to go into the House and commented on the unfortunate relations which had developed between the Government and the Press since my retirement in 1947. I told Mr Morrison that the newsprint supply position for which I had been responsible in the War was alarming and that the Government should, I thought, take some initiative; but that Mr Harold Wilson was not the person to do it. Mr Morrison agreed.

He went on to say that he had read my book and would like me to tell him about it. I did so over lunch. Morrison listened carefully and expressed a large measure of agreement with the points I made. He asked if I had applied my ideas to the nationalised industries. I replied in the negative, but added that I thought the ideas applicable to that sphere, but did not know enough about the nationalised industries to be able to make a sufficiently valuable contribution to the discussion. On the way back to the House of Commons Mr Morrison asked me if I would accept a position on one of the nationalised industries as a part-time director, which I said would be rather difficult to combine with my other work. He said he would like to have me in the House of Commons, but I did not react to this, except to say I thought it important the ideas in the book should appear in a neutral atmosphere before they were taken up by any particular party, and I thought my ideas should be made known among business people and the Churches so as to mobilise non-political opinion. Finally Mr Morrison asked if I would talk to his research people and I said I would gladly do so, and also promised to send him a copy of my articles in the *Fabian News*, and in the *Christian Newsletter* on relations with the Press, which we had also discussed.'

A week later I was asked to go and see Patrick Gordon Walker, Secretary of State for Commonwealth Relations. My note on this conversation is as follows:

'Mr Walker said that he had been sent a note by Herbert Morrison asking him to see me and said he understood I had been writing an interesting book. I outlined the subject matter and he then said that he was thinking along the same lines. It was clear by what he said that he had given a good deal of thought to the subject and was in agreement that the way forward was for private companies to be made responsible to the community and to the consumer, rather than by action taken by the centre to control industry from outside its structure. He thought the consumer was in danger of being overlooked altogether and described the difficulty of safeguarding consumers. He thought that the main difficulty that would arise was with the trade unions. They are dead against co-operative schemes in industry, or anything smacking of co-partnership. He thought the legislative phase should come, if possible, after the ideas had had time to filter through industry. If it were possible for industry to establish the right to make the workers members of the company, this would be better than asking Parliament for an Act. He agreed that the State would ultimately have to determine the point at which a minimum level of responsibility would become statutory, but he thought that many companies might be willing to move along this line if only to avoid direct control by Government. He was of the opinion that this development was a long term development and would take some years to get established and that meantime the unions would be inclined to look at it with suspicion, but he was convinced personally that the lines of advance lay in the direction of recognising and developing the corporate personality of the company. I asked him who in the Labour Party were thinking on these lines. He said very few; he named Austen Albu and Jack Diamond, and I mentioned that I had considered collaborating with Albu in writing my book, but we had thought it best to publish separately. He agreed it would be more valuable to have a completely independent study and said he would like to see the book as soon as possible, which I promised he would do.'

Patrick Gordon Walker was evidently one of the brains of the Labour Party who was being groomed for a higher position. It struck me that he had been given an easy job so he could do some thinking with an eye on the future. What I liked about him was his acceptance of the idea that so revolutionary a doctrine as I was putting forward could only be accomplished over a period of years and there would have to be a pre-political stage of public discussion before legislation would be practicable. I thought in this respect he was being realistic without being uninterested and he appeared to me a person with insight. He thought the Aneurin Bevan school of thought was completely impracticable and that the toughest problem of labour looking ahead was to convince the unions of the need for investing industry with a greater degree of corporate personality. The unions were in danger of becoming undemocratic owing to their compulsory powers over labour, in fact he wanted me to write a second book on the machinery of the trade unions, which is evidently something to which the Government are giving thought. (My book *The Responsible Worker* was published in 1975.)

I told both Morrison and Gordon Walker (the latter had been Morrison's parliamentary private secretary before being made a Minister) that the reason why nationalisation must fail was because it did not recognise the need for separate representation of the conflicting interests of consumers, the local community, workers and financial controllers. Under nationalisation as conceived by the Labour Party the same people would be required to represent different and conflicting interests. When I said this to Morrison he replied that the government had too little time to think out the theory of nationalisation in advance: they must work out the theory as they went along and correct it as need arose.

In spite of being unwilling to enter politics, where I felt my ideas would become intellectual footballs rather than be thought through, I continued to meet Morrison and we lunched together a number of times during 1951-53. I made a note of one conversation, which took place in the private dining room of the Reform Club. It shows how little had been done to bring capital and labour together in the three years following our first meeting, and how little the Labour government understood nationalisation. By then Morrison had moved on to be Shadow Foreign Secretary. But he was still concerned, as the following shows:

'16 December 1953. Herbert Morrison lunched with me at the Reform Club, together with Tom (now Lord) Williamson and Bob Edwards (now M.P.). The Chairman of the T.U.C., Jack

Tanner, was to have come but cancelled because of the threat of a railway strike.

We talked about nationalisation and private industry and Tom Williamson appealed to Herbert to give up the nationalisation policy and instead to concentrate on finding a way to bring about some measure of public responsibility in industry as a whole. He said he had been advocating a policy for a long time along the lines I suggested in my book. There should be Trustees to look after the interests of the Government, the community and the consumer in public companies, and dividends in those companies should be limited. The Company Acts should be amended.

Morrison responded by throwing the ball back: 'The T.U.C. must give a lead.' But Williamson replied that the T.U.C. could not because of its divisions: the Bevanites were looking back-wards, while others like himself wanted a forward policy. 'Let the T.U.C. appoint a small Committee to develop new thinking; bring it to the Labour Executive when you are ready and we will see it through. There is no practical alternative, but the initia-tive must now come from the T.U.C. We are meeting with Griffiths and one or two members of the General Council to help co-ordinate our plans but let's do it quietly.' Morrison added that he was in full agreement that the Memorandum and Articles of large public companies should be widened to take account of their social obligations.'

The T.U.C. failed to respond to this challenge. What Temple sought and Sam Courtauld advanced, what interested Fleck, and what Herbert Morrison failed to sell to the T.U.C., was how to give large enterprise moral legitimacy. The problem still awaits solution. Privatisation is no more the answer than nationalisation. Both policies omit the human element. Balance and trust is in the long run the only sure foundation of authority.

In June 1947 I had purchased at Sotheby's a copy of Hooker's *Ecclesiastical Polity* 1597, one of the rarest and wisest books in English literature. Hooker shall have the last word on nationalisation.

'Two foundations there are which bear up public societies, the one a natural inclination, whereby all men desire sociable life and

82

fellowship, the other an order... agreed upon touching the manner of their union in living together.'

I shall add one further word about Herbert Morrison for the sake of the record. In the life of Herbert Morrison[*], Hannen Swaffer is given credit for suggesting at the height of the Blitz that Sir John Anderson should be replaced as Home Secretary by Herbert Morrison, who was a cockney and much loved by his fellow Londoners. It happened that I had already made this suggestion to two of my directors, Lord Rothermere, and Lord Southwood (Swaffer's employer) over lunch at the Savoy, adding that having a base – Alford House – in the Lambeth Walk I knew a little of what Lambethians felt about the night bombing. Rothermere and Southwood urged me to put my suggestion to Lord Beaverbrook. After lunch I went immediately to Whitehall where Beaverbrook was conducting a meeting of the Air Marshals: he came out and saw me at once. A week later Herbert Morrison was made Home Secretary.

[*]Donoughue & Jones *Herbert Morrison* Weidenfeld & Nicolson, London, 1973, p. 284

CHAPTER XXI

Geoffrey Keynes & William Blake

Like Leonardo de Vinci, Blake is an artistic polymath. His range is prodigious: poet, painter, engraver, printer, illustrator, and prophet; all these skills placed at the service of an indomitable will to make the ways of God plain to men. Born in obscurity, living in simplicity, dying in poverty, and without formal education, Blake has captured the imagination of the savant and the ordinary public alike. His 'Jerusalem' hymn has become a second national anthem, while his poem 'Tyger Tyger' is said to be the best known poem in the English language.

I was attracted to Blake at a very early age. My father was interested in the Swedish philosopher and seer Emanuel Swedenborg, and we had thirty or more volumes of his at home. In his *Arcana Celestia* Swedenborg reports his journeys to the other world. One of his books has the title *Heaven and Hell* and Blake's version, or parody, is called *The Marriage of Heaven and Hell*. It begins:

'As a new heaven is begun…the Eternal Hell revives. And lo! Swedenborg is the Angel sitting at the tomb: his writings are the linen clothes folded up.' Swedenborg in other words witnessed to Blake the divine humanity of Jesus Christ.

I first met Geoffrey Keynes at a wedding in 1944, but he had already written to me a year previously to ask if I had any original Blakes to be recorded in his forthcoming *catalogue raisonée*. I replied that I owned a proof set of the 21 Job engravings, the 7 Dante engravings and an original watercolour drawing of Elisha begging Elijah to grant him a double portion of his spirit, the spirit of prophecy or imagination.

In the drawing Elisha stands humbly before his mentor asking that he be granted a double portion of Elijah's spirit, while Elijah prepares to take off for the next world in the fiery chariot of his imagination. The subject is quite distinct from the colour print in the Tate Gallery of God judging Adam, with which it has been confused. As Blake himself says: 'This world of imagination is the world of eternity; it is the divine bosom into which we shall all go after the death of this vegetated body.'

Geoffrey is the only Englishman I knew who would greet his male friends with a kiss, and this was typical of his affectionate nature, which was perhaps more readily shown to his friends than to his family. Geoffrey loved accuracy. But he loved friendship even more. Once admitted to the inner circle of his friends one could do, or say, no wrong. One was privileged and able to ask a foolish question without fear of losing face. Geoffrey was a born collector, as his collections in the Fitzwilliam and Cambridge University Library testify. His willingness to pass on informa-tion and his eagerness to correct error were limitless. I felt at times that my lack of knowledge would tell against a friendship I valued highly, but it never did. I loved the man and tried to keep him in my prayers and was happy when, shortly before he died, Geoffrey wrote: 'I find I am ready to believe in Blake's God. And He is the kind of Christian I should like to be.' (31 January 1982)

Geoffrey took me in hand and taught me all I know about Blake. Love of Blake is a great unifier, and our friendship pros-pered. Although he was twenty one years older, we were conge-nial. Geoffrey was a good letter-writer and I possess dozens of letters written in his clear, stylish hand in brown ink. All of them come to the point immediately. A letter from Geoffrey dated 5 May 1946 says:

'How nice you are – although a "business man". Not one of the hard faced sort celebrated by JMK. Anyway I like you very much. But this is really to tell you that I have today seen an entirely new and unrecorded drawing, water colour, by HIM. It has been sent to Christie's… its proper fate would be to be bought by Samuel Courtauld and be given to the Fitzwilliam…

Your affectionate Geoffrey.'

When Paul Mellon bought the only complete copy of Blake's prophetic book *Jerusalem* from Colonel Stirling, Geoffrey looked about for some way of publishing a facsimile in full colour. Arnold Fawcus and the Trianon Press provided the answer, while the will of Graham Robertson in 1948 provided the means. In Geoffrey's account in his autobiography, *The Gates of Memory*, the *Jerusalem* was our first concern. But as early as November 1945 I had written to Dr Tom Jones of the Pilgrim Trust asking if they would help reproduce the Blake *Bible Illustrations*, the drawings for Milton's poems, and *Jerusalem*. Geoffrey saw and approved the letter before I sent it. The reply asked us to wait, and it was another three years before we could get started, and we then concentrated on publishing *Jerusalem*. *The Bible Illustrations* were to follow. There has only been one attempt at publishing a Bible with Blake illustrations. Mrs Ruth Greenough published *The Bible for my Grandchildren* in 1952 in the U.S.A. with thirty two of Blake's Bible illustrations, out of the possible total of 175, of which some may have been lost or destroyed. As I pointed out in an article in the *Blake Quarterly* in Spring 1988, there is still much work to be done by the Blake Trust. The Dante drawings – 102 of them – have not been reproduced in colour to this day.

The William Blake Trust was incorporated on 21 March 1949, Geoffrey leaving me to deal with the legal aspects. Our first Trustees included representatives of the Courtauld Institute, the British Museum Department of Prints and Drawings and the Chairman of the National Art-Collections Fund. We made known the purpose of the Trust in the following words:

'to promote the continued study of Blake and to make his work better known by publishing the finest possible reproductions of his works.'

By 1989 the Trust had completed the *Prophetic Books*, the Dante Engravings, the 21 Job Engravings, the catalogue of Bible Illustrations, the *Songs of Innocence & of Experience*, the illustrations to Gray's *Elegy* and Young's *Night Thoughts*. But the Dante and Milton watercolours have still to be reproduced as well as the Bible illustrations.

CHAPTER XXII

The Great Blake Sale – 22 July 1949

When the celebrated Blake collector Graham Robertson died on 4 September 1948, he had accumulated a third of Blake's watercolours and temperas, having acquired a large part of the Butts collection from Captain Butts' grandson. Blake lovers will recognise Captain Butts as Blake's most generous and constant supporter.

On 22 July 1949 there took place at Christie's 'the greatest Blake Sale that has ever taken place or ever will' (Geoffrey Keynes' introduction to the sale catalogue). The first 48 items were paintings and watercolours of Biblical subjects, the remaining 42 lots being mostly pencil drawings and sketches.

Right up to the eve of the sale it appeared likely that the best things – and they included some of Blake's greatest religious paintings – would go abroad, the Americans in particular being partial to Blake. Behind the scenes in London there was feverish activity. After others had failed, Pat Macleod, Arnold Fawcus' young partner, succeeded at the last minute in persuading Graham Robertson's executor Kerrison Preston to allow some of the estate to be used to buy Blake pictures for the nation. An urgent meeting was called between the Trustees of the Tate Gallery and the William Blake Trust, and seven paintings and watercolours were provisionally earmarked for purchase for the Tate. Maximum reserves were placed on each item, ranging from £500 to £5,000. Only three pictures in the sale had higher reserves and they were purchased for the National Gallery of Scotland, the Tate Gallery, and the British Museum. Of the 48 most important pictures in the sale the William Blake Trust, through the National Art-Collections Fund, bid for 20 items of which they secured 18, the other two being purchased by Gerald Agnew for the Victoria & Albert Museum.

Thus the national institutions were given 20 of the finest Blakes in return for which the Trustees and Director of the Tate undertook to upgrade their exhibition of William Blake's pictures to reflect the fact that they now had one of the best, if not *the* best, Blake collection in the world.

Before the sale some of the William Blake Trustees met at Christie's and surveyed all 48 lots to decide which would most suitably be bought for the Nation and which to let go to private buyers and other museums. As we limited our bidding to 20 items it meant that 28 others were available to anyone who cared to bid for them.

The American museums and galleries pooled their bids and entrusted them to Dr Rosenbach, who was elderly, tired after a long Atlantic flight, and hard of hearing. He only bought one drawing. Gerald Agnew sat beside me with my wife and father on my other side. The first item 'God Blessing the Seventh Day' was bought by Gerald for me. Later in the sale I was able to buy 'The Flight into Egypt' and 'Christ the Mediator', two of Blake's finest temperas. I was astonished that the 'experts' (including Lord Crawford, Croft-Murray of the British Museum, Anthony Blunt and Geoffrey Keynes) passed over these pictures, especially the 'Flight into Egypt' which Roger Fry has described in detail in his book *Vision and Design*[*] contrasting it with Giotto's version of the same subject. Incidentally this was the sole occasion in my life on which I borrowed money. Staying with my parents the night before the sale, I wished aloud that I had £2,000 to spare. Without a minute's hesitation my father said 'I will lend you £2,000'. Not only that; he came to the sale. We got all three Blakes we wanted for less than £2,000 and I shall always be grateful to my father for his instantaneous generosity and trust.

[*] Roger Fry, Harmsworth, 1961, p.174

CHAPTER XXIII

Billy Graham & the Editors

I was asked to be Chairman of the Publicity Committee for Billy Graham's visit to England in 1955. In view of my close association with the British Press during the War I thought it would be helpful to arrange a meeting for the twenty-one editors of the national newspapers to meet Billy Graham. I was warned in advance that editors do not like to meet their editorial rivals, for fear of attracting a uniformity of outlook. But I persisted, wrote to every editor personally, and had eighteen acceptances and only three refusals. We lunched on 12 May at the Waldorf Hotel with sixteen editors, two having to fall out at the last minute.

In welcoming the Press I made the following comments: 'As editors you are stewards and practitioners of a mystery or craft, that of editing. Billy Graham is also the master of a craft or Mystery, the greatest mystery of all – religion. I have it on the testimony of a great editor and newspaper man, that if he had his career over again he would like to have been an evangelist. This shows Lord Beaverbrook's grasp of essentials. I won't stand between you and Billy but I wish to welcome you most warmly. If the room is more confined and the board less groaning than usual, it is because I am paying the expenses of this lunch myself and you are all genuinely my guests today. In a small way I have worked with Billy Graham as Chairman of the London Publicity Committee. I have seen the care with which all the arrangements are made and finance administered. I love Billy Graham, because he is bringing something back into English life we had nearly lost: the freshness of an infectious faith; a frank and open declaration of the Gospel of Jesus Christ. Billy Graham, please will you speak to us?'

It was a successful occasion, heightened by the *Mirror* man ordering himself a bottle of gin during the lunch. After drinking half he became decidedly friendly. I had thank-you letters from most of my editorial guests, the editor of the *Star* writing 'revealing and impressive'; the *News Chronicle* 'I was surprised to find how impressed I was by him'.

What pleased the editors was Billy's frankness, allied to charm and gaiety. He dealt fairly with every question put to him, including some rude ones, and obviously enjoyed himself.

CHAPTER XXIV

Church Assembly

CANON LAW AND SYNODICAL GOVERNMENT

My first speech in the Church Assembly was made on my forty-first birthday, 22 June 1949. It called for a statement showing the total financial resources of the Church. We had found in visiting the parishes in Oxford diocese that there was much confusion as to the real position, which needed to be cleared. After debate my motion was approved. On the same day the Assembly called for a report on the effects, personal and social, of gambling. When this report was presented to the full Assembly a year later, it failed to condemn gambling as a practice and took a soft line. I rose to ask that the report be rejected, quoting William Temple's 'the distribution of money by chance is a socially wrong principle.' My own ground was that I found it impossible to reconcile trust in luck with belief in Providence. The debate raged all day. In the end the Assembly passed a motion declaring its conviction that the Report 'was not fully representative of the mind and conscience of the Church of England as a whole' which was as good as a rejection of an Assembly report, a rare event. When the debate was over the Archbishop of Canterbury, Dr Fisher, came down to the body of the hall and congratulated me.

As a result of that debate, which the *Manchester Guardian* described as one of the most important debates ever to have taken place in the Assembly, I was invited to stand for the influential standing committee consisting of the two archbishops and 18 or so bishops and senior laymen. I duly stood, was elected, and remained on the Standing Committee, as it was called, for the next 15 years.

It also led to the BBC asking me to be guest speaker in the Home Service on 'Gambling – social menace or harmless diversion'. I ended my opening statement as follows:

'Gambling substitutes a passing excitement in something over which we have no control for the adventure of living a full life. It gives us an itch instead of a purpose.'

I still believe this to be true.

Following Parliament's rejection of the 1928 Prayer Book Measure, an influential section of the Clergy determined to revise the canon law of the church as a prelude to seeking a greater degree of self government. Already in 1935 a Commission set up by the archbishops had recommended that 'the freedom of legislation without recourse to Parliament which is possessed by the established Church of Scotland should be sought for the Church of England also.'

A necessary step towards self government was to involve the Laity in revising the canon law of the church which had been the same since 1603. On 18 June 1951 the two archbishops came down to the House of Laity, then in session, to ask for the Laity's cooperation in revising the canons. The archbishops pointed out that the Laity had no status in the matter. But they proposed, as an act of grace, to invite the cooperation of the House of Laity. I disagreed, but said nothing, because I had put down a motion on the subject which was to be debated two days later in full Assembly. It welcomed the revision of the Canons, which was in itself non-controversial. But what I went on to say *was* highly controversial. I sought to demonstrate that the concurrence of the Laity in church legislation was essential, being a Biblical principle of great antiquity and significance. I quoted Archbishop Benson's *Life of Cyprian* which showed the Laity playing their full part in church government in the third century A D, and from a document known as the Report of the Convocations on the position of the Laity in the Church. Published in 1902 it concluded:

'We perceive very clearly…that the ultimate authority and the right of collective action lie with the whole body, the church.'

This document had gone out of print and it took some time to discover a copy. I asked the Archbishop of Canterbury to allow the 1902 Report to be reprinted. Leave was at first refused but eventually given and the report was published by the Church

Information Board with an introduction by Professor Norman Sykes which came out strongly in favour of coordinate government by the clergy and laity acting together.

In my speech of 20 June 1951 to the full Church Assembly, I advanced four principles which I thought should govern revision of the canons.

1. The laity should be accorded their scriptural and proper rights of agreement and dissent.

2. The canons should not bind unnecessary burdens on the laity. There should be a canon of charity, as proposed by Cranmer in 1537.

3. The passing of new canons must mean that the clergy accept law-abidingness as a principle.

4. Nothing in the canons should militate against reunion.

In the ensuing debate the Bishop of Chichester endorsed my four principles and prophesied that the debate that day might prove to be of historic importance. The Archbishop of York, speaking as Chairman of the Commission on Canon Law, said that he could vote wholeheartedly for the motion and accept every one of the points I had made. The Archbishop of Canterbury said the debate, which lasted all afternoon, had been 'extraordinarily useful' and one of the most enjoyable to which he had ever listened. At the end of the debate my motion was carried without opposition, and with the thanks of the chair. It was a day made possible for me by years of preparatory reading in which my book collecting had played a significant role. Another of my sources was Bishop Gore's *Essays in Aid of the Reform of the Church 1902*, particularly the opening essay in which he writes:

'Nothing can be more important than to establish this proposition – that the proposal to coordinate laity with clergy in the government of parishes, dioceses and provinces is not a revolutionary measure but demonstrably a return to the original Christian Ideal.' (p.8)

I believe the battle for synodical government was won that day, although it would take another nineteen years for it to be enshrined in the law. Hugh Craig identifies the beginning of the 'long haul to Synodical government' with my speech of 11 February, 1953, in the Assembly*. But the case for full lay participation in the work, witness and administration of the Church was made, and accepted by the bishops, clergy and laity of the Church Assembly, on 20 June, 1951. The precise form in which the laity should in future be associated with the Clergy in the government of the Church would be the subject of prolonged discussion, and after twenty years of experiment, the coordination of clergy and laity in the government of the Church of England is still in the experimental stage. But the sheer effort of bringing established ways under critical judgment has created a new and welcome sense of partnership, without which the Church would be fatally handicapped.

As a result of making the speech which led to synodical government, I was drafted on to the Canon Law Revision Committee where the Canons of 1603 were being scrutinised one by one and rewritten by a select band of bishops and senior clergy together with a few legally minded laymen. Most of the canons are about the forms of service and the duties of the clergy, but a few directly concern the laity, notably those on marriage and re-marriage, admission to communion, baptism, and the representation of the laity in the government of the church.

In 1955 the Archbishop asked me to go to the Second World Ecumenical Conference at Evanston as a delegate of the Church of England. The theme was reunion. While the discussions went on the Anglican church would not admit non-member communicants as of right, but only as of grace.

I thought, reading the Caroline divines Richard Baxter and George Herbert, that this 'fencing of the altar' was wrong, and said so in a speech I made, or attempted to make, in the Church Assembly on the 14 June 1955. I believed we could safely admit the logic of the historical witness of what was known as 'occasional conformity'. The Archbishop intervened half way through my speech and said it was out-of-order. I attempted to continue, but

*The Synod of Westminster, SPCK, London, 1986, page 25

94

the Assembly showed they had had enough. So I sat down. But the result of the Archbishop's intervention was that the speech was printed in full in the Church press and reported in the national press, which brought the subject into the limelight, the exact opposite of the Archbishop's intention.

The prohibition of second marriages in Church proved to be another thorny question. Here the suggestion of Christopher Chavasse, Bishop of Rochester, seemed to present the best solution: namely to allow a service in church, not the ordinary marriage service, but a service of penitence, in which the congregation accepted a degree of responsibility, alongside that of the couple being married. I came to love Bishop Chavasse and we saw eye to eye on most things. He asked me to be a trustee of his new college at Oxford, St Peter's Hall, and I was happy to accept. With the passage of time I became the senior trustee, my only duty now being to help nominate the Visitor, where previously the trustees appointed the Master.

The revision of the Canons took twenty-two years (1947-69) but I left the committee in 1964. Canon Alec Vidler, editor of *Theology* and Dean of King's College, Cambridge, and a much loved friend, in a letter to *The Times* of 18 May 1957 attacked the whole process of canon law revision as a 'waste of time.' But I think this is unfair. It had become necessary to restore order in the Church of England. The canons are laws of the Church. Their scope is indicated by my letter to the Archbishop of 6 April 1964 which will be found in appendix.

Revision of canon law had the merit of alerting members of the Church of England to the fact that their rights were at risk and might be lost. As drafted, the canons left no place in the government of the church for the laity. My reading in ecclesiastical history, particularly Bishop Gore's *Essays on Church Reform*, and above all the 1902 Report of the Convocations on the position of the laity in the Church, convinced me that the freedoms campaigned for by William Temple in the 1930s through the Life and Liberty Movement were in danger. A danger on the other side was that of rule by church parties. Votes in the Assembly on constitutional questions like the participation of the laity in church government were apt to follow party lines – catholic, evangelical or liberal. So it was decided to set up a strong non-party group (realising that we were guilty of a misnomer) and I agreed to act as its convener. We intended having joint meetings with a similar number of MPs who were Anglicans and shared our concern. I wrote to Quintin Hogg, later Lord Hailsham, on 4 March 1955 setting out our aims, and a similar letter was sent to a dozen other MPs, who agreed to meet us. We first dined at the office of PEP (Political and Economic Planning) but found that a three line whip was always likely to interrupt our proceedings. So we dined instead at the House of Commons. Among the Parliamentarians who accepted our invitations were Lord Hailsham, Lord Caldecote, Eric Fletcher, Richard Wood, Henry Brooke, Spencer Summers, Lancelot Joynson-Hicks and J. E. Simon Q.C. When we met on 7 February 1956 we were eight a side. I wrote a memorandum for the occasion: 'Changing Relations of Church and State', for circulation to the members. In this I stressed the historic importance of the alliance between church and state, and the need for positive action to maintain it. The reaction of our parliamentary friends was mixed. Lord Hailsham told me that Parliament was no longer either willing or able to represent the Anglican laity. Enoch Powell, at a meeting in the House of Commons, took an eccentric line by saying that synodical government would not work until there was corruption in the election of its officers and representatives. At the time I was shocked, but I think today I can see what he was driving at. As for Lord Hailsham's fears, Parliament has since the introduction of synodical government in 1970 spent at least one night debating whether divorced clergy should be allowed to continue to hold office, while the Ecclesiastical Committee of Parliament still occasionally considers questions relating to church and state relations. What we were after was to alert MPs to the danger of the existing church-state relationship being undermined through negligence or pressure of other claims on Parliament's time. I believe we succeeded in this limited aim.

In addition to promoting synodical government, sitting on the canon law revision committee, and serving as a member of the powerful standing committee, I was asked, in May 1959, to help set up a Church Information Board (CIB) and to be its first chairman. The object was to establish closer links with such organisations as the press and BBC, and to keep the Archbishops 'informed of the movements of public opinion'. My first task was to appoint a chief information officer. My choice fell on Colonel Robert Hornby, an officer serving with the Far East land forces in Singapore. We negotiated by telephone line to Singapore, and Robert agreed to come to us by the end of the year. It turned out to be a happy choice. Colonel Hornby showed himself a master craftsman in the art of publicity. In William Purcell's biography* Dr Fisher praises the work of the CIB in general, and of Robert Hornby in particular, in glowing terms. Dr Fisher was an enthusiast for public relations. He even allowed his public utterances to be vetted in advance by Colonel Hornby, and invited me to come to Lambeth Palace whenever the need arose.

I came to know Dr Fisher well and admired him. He treated me rather like a headmaster might treat his senior prefect (he had been headmaster of Repton). I received many letters from him on doctrinal subjects connected with canon law revision, some of great length. We frequently differed, but in the end Dr Fisher usually carried the day, just because he was prepared to argue the case out. When he retired, in February 1961, I wrote him a short note. His reply written in his own hand, touched me: 'I value very greatly so generous a message from an old and faithful sparring partner – never without profit in the end'.

I occasionally made verbatim notes of interesting conversations with interesting people. One such took place in May 1956 in the course of a lecture at which the Archbishop was in the Chair. This is my note exactly as I recorded it.

'Professor Norman Sykes gave his lecture today at Lambeth Palace on Cranmer. Several of my books were on exhibition. About 300 (people) present, predominantly lay. At the close the Archbishop commented freely.

*Fisher of Lambeth, Hodder & Stoughton, London 1969, page 254

"You will notice," he said "that at the Reformation the Laity opposed the Clergy and the opposition has continued until today. You will see the Canons were to be revised at the Reformation and that Cranmer actually produced a version. We are at it again now. But Parliament cannot now, as then, represent the Laity. So we find the Laity quite rightly demanding a full voice in Church government. And we have set up a Royal ... no, a learned ... Commission to advise us. I think they are having difficulty ... but the problem is one that we have inherited from the Reformation and we still have to find the solution. Then there are the marriage laws. Cranmer drafted new Canons for marriage, and now we are engaged on the same task. The State, then as now, provides the framework and sets the limits of our endeavours. I have never thought it a bad thing or felt we were really hampered by the State connection. The Church we have; its liturgy, homilies, articles, ordinal and collects, are Cranmer's. He is the Architect of our reformed Church, and we can thank God for it."

Afterwards I spoke to the Archbishop. "Hello, I didn't see you" he says. "How are you getting along in the Synodical Government Commission?" Before answering this question I said "Your Grace's remarks at the close interested me most of all."

The Archbishop: I was batting on your wicket, wasn't I, Goyder?

GG: Very much so.

Archbishop: And how is it going in Commission?

GG: Slowly. Manchester wanted to abolish Convocation, Exeter and Eric Kemp oppose it. Sir Thomas Barnes has worried about the constitutional changes and consequent legislation but is coming round.

Archbishop: It is slow work, I hear.

GG: Yes, but mainly because the Chairman (Dean of Christ Church) went to America for nearly a year.

Archbishop: Are you coming out somewhere?

GG: Yes. I think we will recommend a voluntary joining of Laity to Convocations. If we also remove the bar from discussing doctrine in the Assembly the way is open for the slow assimilation of the two bodies. Neither will want to be jettisoned, so let's bring them closer together and gradually put business where it can best be done – liturgical and theological in Convocation, administration and finance in the Assembly and assimilate the two?

Archbishop: That seems right. Did you hear Sykes' opening quotation from Fuller about the nail driven too hard splitting the wood?

GG: No, but I happened to read his last quotation from Fuller's *Holy State* before retiring last night.

Archbishop: I must get the quotation from Sykes about the nail. You are right to move slowly. That is the English way.

GG: My only fear is for your Grace's health.

Archbishop: I am in very good health.

GG: But we shall need you for another twenty years.

Archbishop: Not so long as that.

Afterwards –

Norman Sykes, sourly, to me: Always the Archbishop will make his speech afterwards.

GG: But it was a good one and helpful to us.

Sykes: You must be present at the next Commission. The Dean [of Winchester] tried to wreck the last.

GG: I intend to be there.

Sykes: Unfortunately I can't go.'

In July 1961, Michael Ramsey succeeded Dr Fisher as Archbishop of Canterbury. His style was altogether different. Whereas Dr Fisher was prepared to be advised, Dr Ramsey was unwilling to give time to the promotion of the church's message through the agency of public relations. His view, which he expressed strongly to me, was that the Church Information Office was a piece of machinery, to be used at the Archbishop's discretion. After being twice by-passed in important communications to Parliament while heading an office that was responsible to the Assembly for Church information, I decided to resign.

Robert Hornby resigned at the same time (November 1964) without giving his reasons. I have no doubt frustration was a contributory cause.

My simultaneous resignation from the Church Information Board and from the Standing Committee, the latter after four-teen years continuous membership, was intended as a protest that the Committee under Dr Ramsey's leadership was in danger of becoming a creature of the bureaucracy instead of a free standing policy-making body. I was in a strong position as I had recently come near the top in the election of lay members of the Assembly to the Standing Committee.

Dr Ramsey sent for me and asked me why I had resigned from the Standing Committee. I am afraid he was annoyed and showed it. But I felt someone must question the direction in which we were going and I said so. For one thing the church secretariat had without consultation divided the Standing Committee in two so that it now met only four times a year under the Archbishop's chairmanship instead of eight. For another, the officials had decided, without prior consultation, on a ten minute limit on speeches in the Assembly which I regarded as a retrograde step in the battle for synodical government. Ten minutes is long enough for a comment, but not long enough for stating a case. My resig-nation from the Church's 'cabinet' and from the chairmanship of the department of information was widely reported in the press, and created something of a sensation at the time *The Times* 4 November 1964, page 7, *Church Times* 6 November 1964 (front page). The truth is that my interests were developing in other directions and I was growing impatient with the delays in intro-ducing synodical government.

CHAPTER XXV

CIB & CBE

One of the outstanding men of my generation was the Reverend Max Warren, General Secretary of the Church Missionary Society. In 1952 he asked me to help him create a college for briefing men and women for overseas service. The idea came from Harry Holland, the medical missionary, whose father had also been a medical missionary. With help from the British Council the courses began in a small way in 1954, at Moor Park. By 1959 we were briefing 500 men and women a year and were looking for larger premises. Fortunately the Bishop of Guildford then decided to vacate Farnham Castle because of expense, and the possibility of taking it over from the Church Commissioners arose. Permission had however to be obtained from the Church Assembly, and some of the Clergy opposed the idea. I made a speech which included a message from the Prime Minister, Harold Macmillan, received that day. I do not know who drafted the message, but it read as follows:

'Every year thousands of men and women go to live and work overseas. Whatever job they do, they also represent our country, our way of life, our Christian civilisation. That is why Church, State and Business have combined to create and support Overseas Service. Its purpose is to provide information, help and guidance to those who represent us in this way. I warmly commend to British employers and their staffs the courses and facilities which this organisation provides.'

With this timely hint the assembled Clergy voted in favour of the Farnham Castle Measure on 16 February, 1960. Thirty years later we were still at Farnham, now known as the Centre for International Briefing (CIB), with an intake of 1,500 to 2,000 men and women a year and an international reputation. I was an original Director (1962) and Chairman of the Governors from 1969-1977.

In 1972 we decided we needed someone with top level diplomatic experience to represent us at high governmental levels. The choice fell on Lord Howick, and he accepted. But following his untimely death after a climbing accident on the steep crags of Howick, Roger Makins (Lord Sherfield) took his place. Roger had a brilliant career in diplomacy and had been our ambassador in Washington. What I remember most about him is his tremendous laugh and infectious sense of fun. He would bring distinction to any organisation, and we were lucky to get two such men as Lord Howick and Lord Sherfield to be our successive presidents. On his retirement in 1985 Roger wrote me a note about our common concerns: 'I think that together we did a good job in building up the BNAC – though you did all the work! I do hope that the Farnham Castle operation will survive... In retrospect, I don't think anyone has twisted my arm more successfully than you!' Roger was vice-chairman of the British North American Committee at the time he wrote this letter. (I describe the work of the BNAC in Chapter XXVIII.)

In 1976 I received the honour of the CBE, thirty years after my brother Cecil had received the same honour for his work in creating the Indian broadcasting system. I am not sure which of my activities was being recognised but it could have been partly the Centre for International Briefing and partly the British North American Committee.

Both the CIB and the BNAC are educational bodies and brought me in closer touch with that world. I was made a member of the governing board of my old school, Mill Hill.

I was still eagerly collecting rare and important books, although when we eventually moved from our spacious home in Oxfordshire to Suffolk I had to sell some 200 for which there was too little space. The senior London bookseller Alan Thomas, in his catalogue 44 (1982), described my collection as 'The finest library of sixteenth century theology of our time.' The books I sold in April 1979 included the only known copy of the *Book of Common Prayer*, 16mo, 1572; the first edition in English of Calvin's *Institutes* 1561; Queen Elizabeth's original *Proclamation forbidding*

Ministers to Preach 1558; John Foxe's *Acts and Monuments*, first edition, 1563, which had belonged to John Burns; Marbecke's first *Concordance of the English Bible* 1550; Queen Mary's *Proclamation against Heretical Books* 1555 (only one other copy recorded) and a fourth Folio Shakespeare, 1685. (The London Library has a copy of the Sotheby's sale catalogue of 2 November 1979.)

That still left me with over half my collection of early English books. It was a grief to have to part with the others but, with a large family, circumstances required the occasional sacrifice. Thus my beautiful copy of William Blake's *Songs of Innocence and of Experience* (now owned by Paul Getty Jr) was sold for family reasons, while on 23 June 1958 Sotheby's had sold my collection of early English Bibles which enabled us to build a house on our land for my parents in their old age. Sothebys produced a special catalogue for the sale and wrote in the preface:

'The earliest English Bibles have become so rare in recent years that it would be extremely difficult today to form a collection at all comparable with the one now offered. All the versions before the Authorised of 1611 are represented in it.'

This Bible sale was historic, if only because it included William Tyndale's *Pentateuch* of 1530-34 of which only a handful of copies survive. Lovett (*The English Bible in the John Rylands Library*, 1899) describes this book as : 'The rarest and most precious book in the whole series of printed English Bibles or portions of scripture.'

I should myself have thought this verdict more applicable to Tyndale's *New Testament*, an early copy (1536) of which I still possess.

CHAPTER XXVI

The Responsible Company

By 1960 my book *The Future of Private Enterprise* had gone out of print a second time and Basil Blackwell gave me the option of a third edition or a new book. I chose the latter, and *The Responsible Company* came out in November 1961, eighteen months after the appointment by the British Government of a committee – known as the Jenkins Committee – to look into the working of the 1948 Companies Act. Among the members of Lord Jenkins' Committee was Professor Jim Gower, whose book *Modern Company Law* (1954) has become a standard text book on the subject. In his book Gower makes several references to *The Future of Private Enterprise*, both in the text and in the accompanying notes. I was invited to give evidence to the Committee, no doubt through Jim Gower's agency.

At this point I sought the help of friends in drafting a suitable document to send in as evidence. Among those who helped were Professor Allan Flanders of Nuffield College, Oxford (he and I were later to go to India for a conference on the social responsibility of business), Bernard Miller, chairman of the John Lewis Partnership, and Michael Huxley, the founder and editor of the *Geographical Magazine*. The resulting document is reproduced as an appendix to *The Responsible Company*. In the words of *The Times*' Labour Correspondent, writing on 18 July 1960:

'Among those who have given evidence to the Jenkins committee on company law is Mr George Goyder whose book *The Future of Private Enterprise* attracted much attention in 1951. Mr Goyder wants the law changed to make provision for the election of workers to the membership of a company, for the establishment of Trusts in shares on behalf of the employees, and for the creation of a new class of limited liability company with directors representing the consumers, the workers, and the community, as well as the shareholders.

These proposals arise from the view that the exclusive owner-ship of a company by shareholders is becoming an anomaly, that it is contrary to natural justice for such ownership to be perma-nent, and that in the interest of industrial peace and national well-being, public limited liability companies should be made at least to some extend accountable to the workers, consumers, and community.'

Jim Gower sent a copy of my evidence to Lord Denning, who replied: 'I feel that George Goyder and his friends have hit upon one of the real problems which face us in the coming years, which is to adapt the company law system so that it can form its social responsibilities.'

Another interested party was Sir Alexander Fleck, chairman of ICI, Britain's largest company. He and his deputy chairman Sir Raymond Street gave me lunch at the Savoy to discuss my book as it related to ICI. Afterwards Fleck wrote saying he had 'a tremendous lot of sympathy' with what I sought.

The Press, as usual, were helpful. *The Guardian* said of the book and its author (20 November 1961): 'He points out that private enterprise and nationalisation have each failed to meet men's inner needs for participation, status and significance at work,' while *The Director* commented (June 1962): 'A wide ranging and attractive elaboration' of the theme of social responsibility including the evidence submitted to the Jenkins Committee.'
William MacIntyre in the *British Weekly* (15 March 1962) went overboard:

'With a total absence of technical or any other kind of jargon, he states his thesis with great clarity and conciseness and an inescap-able sense of urgency... Mr Goyder has not been content merely to write another book... he has submitted the thesis of his book and his practical proposals to the Jenkins Company Law Committee... In this book we see the mind of a Christian man bringing the Christian doctrine of God and man and his factual knowledge into contact with each other and seeking right judgements that lead to constructive proposals... an excellent example of how Christians should address themselves to the problems of our time.'

Allan Flanders wrote in *Socialist Commentary* (January 1962) commenting: 'What he has to say is the product of careful study and mature reflection, fired by moral purpose. It is a better book in many ways than his earlier *The Future of Private Enterprise* (1951) which it is intended to replace.'

An unnamed correspondent in the *Church of England Newspaper* (6 October 1962) wrote: 'One of the most significant Evangelical developments of our Time, deserving to rank with the vast output of Biblical and Theological literature.'

I also wrote a number of articles on 'The Responsible Company' which were published in *The Times*, the *Observer* and the *Banker*.

One reaction to *The Responsible Company* came from India. Jayaprakash Narayan, a disciple of Gandhi who refused to be President of India, wrote inviting me to come to India and present my views on the social responsibilities of business to a representative gathering over a week in March 1965. Allan Flanders and Ernest Bader were also invited.

In his introductory speech, replying to the Prime Minister's remarks which opened the conference, Jayaprakash said that Gandhi had hoped his theory and practice of Trusteeship might be a gift that India could make to the world. He could hardly have foreseen the neglect and scorn the idea would meet with in independent India. At this point, said Jayaprakash, he was lent a copy of *The Future of Private Enterprise* and its sequel. The Prime Minister (Mr Shastri) was at that time Minister for Commerce and Industry. 'I took the liberty of sending him the material.' This led to a decision to mount a full scale conference to discuss the principles and practice of Trusteeship in business.

The proceedings of the conference were recorded and published in book form in 1966 by Manaktalas of Bombay under the title *The Social Responsibilities of Business*. This book contains the complete text of the statement issued at the close of the conference which Allan Flanders and I drafted under the helpful but critical eye of Jayaprakash, who showed himself to be a veritable saint in the course of the five days conference. Always conciliatory, never raising his voice, always on hand and seemingly invisible, the conference, thanks to him, was a considerable success. One result was that the chairman of the largest company in India – Tata – resolved to introduce a social audit (the idea is discussed in Chapter 17 of *The Responsible Company*). As a result Tata won the Indian Government's permission to increase the dividends paid to the ordinary shareholders!

I have already mentioned Ernest Bader. His pioneer work in founding the Scott Bader Commonwealth had by 1965 made him famous. The story of our friendship has been told in Susanna Hoe's excellent book*. What happened was that one afternoon in 1950 Ernest walked into my office at 18/20 Pall Mall, held up a copy of the *Fabian News* of November 1949 and said: 'I want to set up my business on your principles – will you help me?' This was the beginning of a friendship that never lapsed.

Bader was Swiss, with an intensity of temperament fashioned by living at high altitudes, physical and spiritual. I too am partly Swiss, and partly Welsh. It is an emotional mixture, but one likely to be sympathetic to an idealist like Ernest Bader. Ernest subsequently told me that what first gave him the idea of handing over his business to his employees was reading my article in the *Fabian News* for November 1949 entitled 'Socialism and Private Industry: A New Approach'. This was in fact my first public statement wherein I declared my belief that business 'is naturally a partnership involving four distinct parties' and stated my conviction that at a certain stage in the evolution of every large company 'control on behalf of the owners of share capital should give place to control in the interests of all the four parties to industry'.

This is what Ernest Bader did. He created a Trust for his employees and endowed it with 90% of the shares in Scott Bader Ltd (the remaining 10% would be given later). The Trust was legally a charity, and distributed profits to good causes in the community.

*The Man who gave his Company away, Heinemann, London, 1978

The formal signature of the documents recording the transfer of share capital in Scott Bader to the employees in Trust took place at a hotel in Cambridge on 28 April 1951 in the presence of 145 of the employees who overnight became proprietors instead of hands. Ernest asked me to be the guest of honour and in my speech I likened the new relationship between the founder and employees to a marriage, in which a man and a woman give themselves to one another in order that new life may be created. At the Silver Jubilee of the company in 1976 I was again the guest of honour and used the same analogy. What had been born in the intervening years was a new concept of a company in which social responsibility is allied to excellence and competitiveness. What I tried on both occasions to convey was the reciprocal nature of human beings and human institutions. It was now up to the employees to assume their share of social responsibility.

Under its new constitution Scott Bader has gone from strength to strength. From time to time Ernest suggested my becoming a Trustee of the Scott Bader Commonwealth, as it is called. But I declined the honour, rightly or wrongly, because I felt that my main concern should – as it is in my books – be with big business and the larger companies, and partly because I felt, and still feel, that the problems of social responsibility demand a solution applicable to the circumstances and needs of the large business. For example, the amortisation of share capital is essential, but in the larger companies it would have to be done gradually, whereas Ernest Bader could transfer his shares overnight.

CHAPTER XXVII

Political Interlude

In 1961 I again became involved in politics, this time with the Liberals. It was ten years since Herbert Morrison had tried to get me to take part in planning the Labour Party's post-war industrial policy, and I had learned that the vested interest of the Trade Unions in bargaining would in the last resort prevent their acceptance of social responsibility as a motive for industrial policy. I thought the Liberals more likely to show an interest in 'The Responsible Company', as they had inherited the so-called 'Yellow Book' of 1928 on 'Britain's Industrial Future', where many of my proposals had been anticipated by men with the authority and experience of Lord Keynes, Lord Stamp and Lord Layton. Thus, when I agreed to become the Chairman of the Liberal Party's Standing Committee on Industrial Affairs I had reason to think we could reach agreement along the lines of the 1928 report, suitably updated. Our terms of reference were 'to study the problems of industrial partnership and to produce a practical polic'.

We met weekly for the next six months and failed to come to a common mind. Two of our number owned family businesses employing twenty to thirty people apiece and they were determined to turn the Party in the direction of workers' control. Others on the Committee were, like myself, more familiar with public companies and their needs. Paradoxically the 1928 'Yellow Book' had both stated the problem which caused our divisions and delivered the solution in a single sentence reading:

'It is eminently desirable that the capital required by industry should to the largest possible extent be drawn from profits, and that as large a share of these re-invested profits as the fair claims of capital permit should be assigned to the brain and hand workers.'

On 2 June 1967 the *Guardian* revealed in an article that we were split over the issue of workers' control and spoke of 'extraordinary bitterness' between those who advocated full workers' control and those who would prefer to see the sharing of control. Neither side would yield and we were in an *impasse* until the advocates of workers' control resigned and went off to join the Labour Party. I decided the time had also come for me to resign as Chairman, and thereby lower the temperature. I stayed on the committee until it had met forty-four times and completed its work and in 1968 published its report *Partners at Work*. To that report I added a short dissenting note stating my conviction that splitting profits with the workers was not the best way of proceeding, but that 'The aim of Liberal industrial policy should be to liberate men at work by providing a form of enterprise that is both socially just and economically practical'.

I had been through an experience that has ever since cautioned me against assuming I was made for a life in politics, and I had learned something about my own limitations.

CHAPTER XXVIII

The British North American Committee

In addressing the Church Assembly I had enjoyed the moral support of Earl Grey of Howick. He was a neighbour of Rosemary's family, the Bosanquets of Rock, and chairman of the House of Laity in the Church Assembly. He treated me like a son, having no son of his own. On one occasion he wrote to Rosemary to tell her that I had been given the biggest ovation that he ever remembered being given to a layman. (I don't remember the occasion.) One day in 1968 Lord Grey's son-in-law Sir Evelyn Baring (later Lord Howick) asked me to dine with him at Brooks's Club. Over dinner he asked if I would take on the job of honorary secretary of a transatlantic body to be set up and known as the British North American Committee. I knew Evelyn slightly – we had played tennis together at Howick – and I admired him. The idea was to create a strong transatlantic body to counter the potential influence of the European Common Market where it might be necessary to keep a balance. Not that we disliked or distrusted the Common Market, but we thought a strong transatlantic bond was a necessary counter-influence and wished to retain the special relationship between Britain, the USA and Canada.

The concept was that of a Canadian friend of mine, R. M. Fowler. He persuaded three well known British diplomats of whom two – Sir Michael Wright and Lord Sherfield – had been ambassadors. The fourth man, Robin Turton, was the father of the House of Commons, while Evelyn Baring (Lord Howick) had been Governor of Kenya in the Mau Mau disturbances and was now chairman of the Nature Conservancy, the Commonwealth Development Corporation and a farmer. I asked him if he would be my chairman if I agreed to take on the job of honorary secretary and he said 'yes'.

Our first meeting to explore the idea of a British North American Committee took place at Ditchley Park from the 21 to 23 of February 1969. In the absence of Lord Howick and Lord Sherfield through illness, Lord Watkinson, a former Cabinet Minister, presided. On the British side we had David Barran and Ernest Woodroofe representing Shell and Unilever, respectively; Vic Feather and Leslie Cannon from the Trades Union Congress; Michael Wright and Robin Turton representing diplomacy; and Leonard Beaton and Peter Jay the press. (I omit titles.) We numbered thirty-eight, of whom half crossed the Atlantic to attend our conference. At the end of the meeting it was decided to go ahead and set up the Committee, each side being responsible for its own finances. My first task was to find a research director. Simon Webley joined us from Reeds and it turned out to be a fortunate choice. From the start we worked together as a team and with our opposite numbers in Washington and Montreal.

To all this my business principals in USA and Canada raised no objection: our business in England – newsprint – was very prosperous and I had in any case to go to Canada and USA frequently on business. The BNAC met in full session twice yearly and alternated its meetings between American and Britain. In between meetings we conducted research and published the results. Lord Howick made an excellent chairman, admired and trusted by everyone. When the Queen bestowed her highest honour, the Garter, upon Evelyn, he, echoing Lord Melbourne, remarked to me 'at least there's no damn merit about it'. Typical of the man!

The early authors of publications for the BNAC included Professor Harry Johnson on the economics of the transatlantic relationship; John Marsh on British entry into the Common Market and its potential influence on British and American agriculture; and David Powell on our responsibilities to help in developing the economies of the Caribbean.

In 1985 the Committee had the honour of being received by Mrs Thatcher at 10 Downing Street. About one hundred members attended. I had by then retired but was introduced to the Prime Minister and outlined to her in a few words the origin and purposes of the committee. Incidentally I mentioned Edward Heath, and after that I didn't think she was listening!

I worked closely with John Miller, my opposite number in Washington D.C. John was also secretary of the National Planning Association and of the Canadian American Committee, a parallel body to the BNAC, so he held an influential position at the heart of American politics. We liked each other from the outset, set up guidelines and rules necessary for a transatlantic organisation, and it worked beautifully. In the twelve years I served as British Secretary I can't recall a serious disagreement.

When I retired from being honorary British Secretary in 1981, I persuaded Henry Hankey, a long standing family friend, and a diplomat, to take my place. He is a son of Lord Hankey who was the secretary of the 1914-18 War Cabinet and is the brother of my old friend Christopher Hankey who is a painter and musician. I was given a present of silver when I retired. But what pleased me most was the speech of Sir Alastair Down, in which he said I had been 'the conscience of the Committee'. I greatly hope this might be true.

CHAPTER XXIX

The People's Church

During my twenty-seven years in the Church Assembly I spoke frequently. I soon learned that the best way to influence the debate was to put down a motion. This gives the speaker priority in time and the opportunity to speak twice; once when introducing his subject and again when summing up the debate. I adopted this tactic when attacking the *New English Bible* (9 November 1961) and when introducing the debates on Canon Law and Synodical Government (20 June 1951 and 11 February 1953). Another debating technique is to put down an amendment referring back an Assembly Report, which is how I tackled the debate on gambling (15 November 1950) which ended in the reference back of an Assembly Report. In the course of my duties as Chairman of the Church Information Board all sorts of questions might be raised in the Assembly which required some answer, often impromptu. Thus, 'Had the Chairman of the CIB listened to such and such a programme on television and did he approve of what was said on the 'New Morality'?'*

When I resigned from the Standing Committee and the Church Information Board in 1964 I became unusually free. It was then that I was persuaded by John Stott to write a book for the Evangelical Fellowship in their 'Christian Foundation' series. I called it *The People's Church*. It is a book of less than 100 pages describing the Church as a fellowship of believers in which the divorce of work from worship is overcome. 'The teaching and application of the law of God needs to be undertaken by the Christian fellowship as a whole... the commandment of God is permission. It differs from all human laws in that it commands freedom.' (quoted on page 56, from Bonhoffer).†

*see *Church Assembly Report of Proceedings*, 8 November 1962, p.755
† D Bonhoffer *Ethics*, SCM Press, London 1955 p.248

Before setting out on the book I wrote to the editor John Stott saying (7 September 1964):

'My approach to the subject would be to show that the laity is in fact the Church and includes the Ministry, or you could say that the laity are that part of the Ministry which are active in the world of ordinary affairs... I see the problem of Church government as primarily that of finding a way of freeing the laity to be the Church.'

Publication was on 4 July 1966, and I understand 20,000 copies were printed and sold. The church papers were favourable. The *Church Times* printed three articles in consecutive issues outlining the book's argument, and in an editorial said:

'Only a study of the whole book can do justice to the balance which the author has carefully tried to keep between the distinct functions of the ordained ministry and the laity, and between law and grace in the gospel.'

The editor of *Theology* also wrote positively: 'It is a plea for a concerted application of Christian minds, lay and clerical...to the Church's first task, which is the exhibition of God's law and love in every activity of life... And who speaks through his pages here? Wycliffe, probably, and Bunyan perhaps, Charles Gore, R. H. Tawney and William Temple certainly.'

It was flattering to have the editor of *Theology* looking for my sources in writing *The People's Church* and true that I had felt especially drawn to R. H. Tawney, William Temple and Charles Gore when thinking about the terms and stratagems needed to achieve Synodical government of the Church. It was also the case that I possessed a fifteenth century copy of Wycliffe's Bible and early editions of many of Bunyan's 60 works, and revered both men as fathers of the Church.

But the strongest influence was that of Thomas Cranmer. In his *Determinations of the Universities on the Royal Marriage* 1531 (STC 14287) he re-states the relevance of the moral law for Christians in these words:

'Christ did not take away the moral law of Moses, but only did declare it more plainly' (page 125B).

As regards the canons, Cranmer in *The Institution of a Christian Man*, 1537 (STC 5164, pages 45-46), declared that canons require the assent of the laity; which to my mind clinched the case for synodical government, once Parliament had relinquished any attempt to draw up a fresh code for the church. Cranmer also proposed (in *The Institution of a Christian Man*, page 46) a canon of charity referring to minor problems of ecclesiastical discipline; he says:

'Surely there is no other obedience required... but that men may lawfully omit or do otherwise than is prescribed... so that they have some good and reasonable cause so to do.'
I tried, and failed, to have this added to the new canons.

With the publication of *The People's Church* in 1966 my career in the Church at the centre came to a natural end. Synodical Government was on its way and was destined to become law in November 1970. Having resigned from the Standing Committee and the Church Information Board I was content to take a back seat. When I spoke, it was to make a point in four or five minutes; not to present a case backed with authority, taking 20 to 30 minutes, as was the case with Synodical Government and the *New English Bible*.

CHAPTER XXX

Special Interest Groups

THE ALL SOULS GROUP ON EDUCATION

It was my good fortune to have been elected a member of a number of special interest groups. One of these was the All Souls Group on Education, which flourished in the 1940s and 50s and had among its members the heads of universities, university colleges and directors of education. We met three times a year under the aegis of Dr W. G. S. Adams, the Warden of All Souls, Sir John Newsom acting as secretary. The group's twenty-first anniversary was held at Magdalen College, Oxford on 23 June 1962. Of the sixty-five members fewer than half a dozen were from the world of business. Among the subjects discussed at our weekend meetings were the aims of education; local government reform with John Maud; religious education in the national curriculum; independence in education with Sir Robert Birley; the new universities with Lord Fulton; education for artists and designers; youth service; health in the community; publicity and public opinion; and so on. To be present and be led by an expert in his own field was an education in itself.

We were a decidedly secular and pragmatic fellowship. Yet underneath the intellectual level one often detected the foundations of a firm Christian faith. Thus Sir John Newsom in a letter to me of 24 December 1963, wrote:

'I do feel desperately sorry for the Church of England at present with its exponents of both "a new Theology" and "a new Morality". Most of what they say and write is, in fact, a repetition of ancient heresies... I always get very suspicious when people begin to explain away sin.'

THE CHRISTIAN FRONTIER COUNCIL

The Christian Frontier Council was another special interest

group and its work has been described in Chapter X I X . I was elected a member in 1941 and took an active part in the meetings for several years. I can remember to this day having to present to the Frontier Council my estimate of William Beveridge's post-war blue print *Full Employment in a Free Society* and how much effort I had to put into mastering my subject. A similar but not quite so daunting experience was when I gave two lectures at King's College London on the social and economic conditions of Palestine in the time of Our Lord, a subject about which I knew absolutely nothing when I accepted, but quite a lot when the time came to lecture! I believe challenges like this should be met, provided there is sufficient time to prepare.

CHRISTIAN TEAMWORK

Another of the special interest groups was known as Christian Teamwork which I helped start in 1957. It owed its foundation to the Reverend Bruce Reed. Our special interest lay in helping to create new organisations with a Christian basis like the Richmond Fellowship for the mentally handicapped, the Langley Fellowship for discharged prisoners and the Abbeyfield Society. The founder of Abbeyfield was Richard Carr-Gomm. I remember his walking into the Christian Teamwork office one day in 1957 and asking for help. He had established in Bermondsey in houses belonging to his family a small hospice type of dwelling where old people could live out their declining years in dignity and comfort and be cared for by a resident housekeeper. Richard's inspiration had a Christian root. In view of its success he wanted to extend the Abbeyfield idea until it became national. Bruce asked me to chair the group to consider with Richard the best way to proceed. We decided we needed to find an administrator. Tommy Frankland had just finished a fundraising exercise for the National Association of Boys' Clubs, and he agreed to come with us full time.

We also needed to find a Chairman. Christopher Buxton recalls that at a Team meeting at the National Liberal Club when various alternative schemes were being discussed, I suddenly said 'Our group must have a Chairman. I intend to do a lot of talking so I don't want to be Chairman. What about Christopher Buxton?' and that was how Christopher became the first Chairman of the Abbeyfield Society, a position which he was to hold for many years, during which Abbeyfield became a national institution.

My one regret is that Tommy Frankland and Richard Carr-Gomm fell out. It is the old story of the administrator versus the conceiver. I believe Voluntary Service Overseas (VSO) suffered in the same way. Alec Dickson was thrown out of the organisation he created, in the interest of 'efficiency'. In Abbeyfield I tried to mediate, along with Robin Turton. But we failed to bring the parties together and this is something I have always regretted. Administrative efficiency is very well, but spiritual efficiency is at least equal in importance and what matters is to create the right relationship between them. This we failed to do. But Richard had the last word when he went off and founded the Carr-Gomm Society.

CHAPTER XXXI

Railway Diversion

On a dark, dank Friday evening in November 1964 I was a passenger in a crowded commuter train made up of multiple diesel units, known to the passengers as 'cattle trucks'. Our coach was chock-full and we stood all the way to Reading. As we passed through Twyford I revolved the idea of addressing my fellow passengers. With only a few minutes to go before our train reached the end of its forty minute journey I suddenly said in a loud voice 'How long are we going to stand this? Who will join me in protesting to British Rail?'

Not a word, not a look, not even the flicker of an eyelid. Passengers might have to put up with discomfort, but they were not prepared to add to it by having to listen to a speech at the end of the day. I was crestfallen.

But hold! Here come two brave men out of the darkness to speak to me on the platform. 'Good show. We will help you and back you. Let's meet and talk it over.' (Both men turned out to be War Office employees.) So we duly met and determined to call a public meeting opposite the station, in the Great Western Hotel. I hired the conference room and told the Press. We expected forty to fifty and ordered coffee for so many although Ralph Cox was pessimistic. 'I think you should be prepared for a very small attendance...people are so anxious to get home' he wrote.

In the event well over two hundred people turned up and we were swamped. A crowd of angry commuters filled the hotel and formed a queue outside in the street which had to be controlled by the police. We took two hundred names and addresses that night and many offers of help and money. A committee of ten was appointed and I was voted Chairman. (We held subsequent committee meetings at Pindars.)

Our policy, or more accurately my policy, ratified by the

committee, was to collect evidence from our three hundred or so members to show up the failures in the service. Almost before we called our second meeting (2 February in Reading Town Hall where there was room for eight hundred) BR had agreed to take off the offending multiple diesel units. In his autobiography Gerard Fiennes, at the time General Manager of the Western Region, admits that the cattle trucks were 'a great stupidity'.

Having collected the facts of delays, breakdowns and inconveniences, we sought to meet the General Manager and his staff to go over the evidence. We did this once a month for so long as it was necessary. We were fortunate in that the BR General Manager at Reading, F. D. Pattisson, was a big man and consistently helpful. As a result of his cooperation we established a friendly relationship in a continuous dialogue. If there was delay due to signal failure, Mr Pattisson would summon before us the BR employee in charge of signalling between Reading and London. If delay was caused by locomotive failure we asked to see the top engineer on the Swindon to Paddington line. We sent to our members a series of bulletins – sixteen of them – giving full information about the progress made in improving BR's service. All the typing and addressing was done by my secretary Miss Eileen Gough and we worked late hours to keep on top.

At the same time we bore down hard on the higher officials of BR. At our first meeting with BR top management in the board room at Paddington we delivered our dossier of operating deficiency in such a determined fashion as to leave the General Manager (in his own words) 'white with anger'.

Our first bulletin (8 January 1965) had clearly set out our policy: 'The patience of the long suffering passengers is exhausted. We must consider what positive action can be taken to compel the railway to give better service. This will mean constant vigilance... and regular reporting to the committee to see that improvements are not only made but maintained.'

One pressure point was to obtain quotations from Reading bus companies willing to provide an alternative to the rail service. This we did. Another was to engage the attention of our three local MPs, whom we met both at the House of Commons and on the platform at Reading Town Hall.

I stayed on as Chairman until 1970 by which time the complaints were only occasional. The campaign for a reasonable commuter service between Reading and London had succeeded although vigilance was still needed.

If the Reading and District Passenger Association (RDPA) was a success it was due to the fact that our members sent in a constant flow of information about train times and delays so that when we met top BR management we very often found we had more, and more accurate, information than they did.

When I retired as Chairman of the RDPA and became its President *honoris causa* the new London divisional manager Mr Todd wrote me a letter in which he said (8 September 1970):

'I would like to congratulate you upon your election to be the President of the Association, which is a fair acknowledgement of the hard work you have done on behalf of the Association and your success in creating a good understanding with us.'

CHAPTER XXXII

St Peter's College, Oxford

I was asked (in 1949) by Christopher Chavasse, Bishop of Rochester, to be one of the four Trustees of St Peter's Hall, Oxford, the other three Trustees being the Bishop of Rochester, the Bishop of Leicester, and Sir Kenneth Grubb. Our duties were not light. We were responsible for the finances of the Hall and for the choosing of its Master. The Hall had been founded by Bishop Chavasse's father and Christopher was for a time its Master. I felt proud to serve St Peter's in this way, as the Hall had a strong sense of evangelical commitment given it by the Chavasse family. Perhaps this same sense of commitment was what enabled Christopher's twin brother to win the Victoria Cross *twice*!

By 1958 we felt the time had come to seek the full status of a university College and we made application to the authorities of Oxford University to that end. The Hebdomadal Council insisted that control of the College and the appointment of its Master be entirely in the hands of the Fellows, subject only to the rights of the Visitor, who would normally be the Bishop of Liverpool. All that was left for the Trustees to do was to suggest the names of a possible Master and to appoint the Visitor. This was acceptable to the Trustees. But the Hebdomadal Council of the University went further. They would not accept any restriction on the choice of Master by reason of his belief, or unbelief. Future masters would no longer have to declare their Christian belief in the terms of the Nicene Creed. The University evidently thought the time had gone when the incoming Master of a College could be required to pass a religious Test. Minute 185 (6 May 1960) of the Hebdomadal Council states that the Committee on Statutes 'object to a religious Test on principle'.

After much reflection I decided I could not with a clear conscience agree to the Committee's requirement. It seemed to me – though not apparently to anyone else – that acceptance of the proposed conditions for the Hall's becoming a full College of the University might involve a breach of trust on my part. It was not as if the College had existed for several centuries. We were an institution founded within living memory by a Christian family for Christian reasons and the Trustees could not escape their responsibility for upholding the purposes of the Hall.

We had reached an impasse, and I was not exactly popular with the fellows or my fellow Trustees. For some weeks I was subjected to intense pressure to give way.

Then a solution occurred to me. I would seek Counsel's opinion of the legality or otherwise of what was proposed. My solicitors, Allen and Overy, recommended John Brunyate, a well known barrister at the Attorney General's office. Within three weeks of being briefed John Brunyate gave his verdict in writing. It said that the Hebdomadal Council must allow the original Christian purpose of the College to stand in its new Charter, but the Master should in future be released from having on his appointment to declare his adherence to the Nicene Creed. It was enough that he subscribed to the original wording of the Trust Deed of 1928.

This compromise satisfied everyone. All the Trustees wrote expressing their gratitude, the Bishop of Rochester's letter being as follows:

'My dear Goyder,
I am very glad you have consulted Counsel and I consider his opinion very valuable. I am sure he is right and that the purposes of the Hall should be set out in full in the Charter and this I know the Hall is prepared to do. If these purposes are set out, and the Trustees can suggest names for a new Master, and the Visitor can veto an unsuitable appointment, I believe we have done all that is possible to preserve the Evangelical tradition of the Hall.'

From then on, the negotiations with the University proceeded smoothly and St Peter's Hall duly became St Peter's College on 22 November 1961. A month later the new College Council elected all four Trustees to honorary fellowship of the College.

There was to be a sequel. Dr Marsh, the Principal of Mansfield, told me he had been much helped by our example in insisting upon retaining the original purpose of the College in our new Charter.

CHAPTER XXXIII

The Responsible Worker

I retired from business in 1973 on reaching sixty-five. But I was almost immediately approached by the industrial editor of Hutchinsons and asked to write a book on industrial relations for their 'Industry in Action' series. I set to work and the book was finished and ready for publication in 1975. Almost at the same time the British Government announced the setting up of a Committee of Inquiry on Industrial Democracy chaired by Sir Alan (afterwards Lord) Bullock. The Bullock Committee asked me to give evidence and I submitted two papers jointly with colleagues who were sympathetic with my ideas for the radical reform of the limited liability company. I wrote both papers. One was signed by John Garnett of the Industrial Society, Sir Bernard Miller of the John Lewis Partnership, and Professor L.C.B. Gower, whose book *Modern Company Law* became a standard text-book and who was among my earliest supporters. The other paper was sent in by request of ICI whose directors told Charles (later Sir Charles) Carter that they preferred the 'Goyder proposals' to any others put forward.

Ever since the publication of Sir William Beveridge's *Full Employment in a Free Society* (1944) successive British governments had sought ways to overcome the hostility of the Trade Unions with their collective memory of massive structural unemployment averaging 14% between 1920 and 1938. Lord Donovan's Royal Commission on Trade Unions had reported in 1968, but when in 1969 the British Government proposed the implementation of his Report including provisions for a compulsory cooling-off period before calling a national strike, the unions were up in arms. They forced the minister – Barbara Castle – to withdraw her White Paper 'In Place of Strife' and effectively ended her political career.

I was not told who it was in Trade Union circles who recommended me to write a book on industrial democracy, but my ideas were by no means hostile to the Trade Unions, as Vic Feather, Sir Leslie Cannon and other leaders of the unions told me when we met under the aegis of the British North American Committee.

Press comments were again favourable, but not so numerous as in the case of my first two books.

The Financial Times wrote (12 December 1975):
'In each of the past two decades George Goyder, a successful industrialist, has presented his credo for business. In the 1950s it was *The Future of Private Enterprise*, followed in the 1960's by *The Responsible Company* in which he argued well ahead of his time the need for social accountability of companies. [It] adds an extra dimension to the debate of worker democracy by suggesting a new structure for the company.'

The Times wrote (15 September 1975): 'The writing is lucid and concise and his arguments avoid technicalities.'

The Responsible Worker was awarded the British Institute of Management's prize of £1,000 for 'the best management book of the year' (1976). We spent the money in Guatemala seeing the Mayan remains.

With the publication of *The Responsible Worker* I felt my public work was over. In the 25 years from 1950 to 1975 I had written three times urging the reform of British company law; I had also published 'the People's Church' (1966) urging the case for a new form of partnership between clergy and Laity. This latter book was to play a small part in preparing the Church of England for synodical government, which came in 1970 with the inauguration of the National Synod by the Queen in Westminster Abbey, less than 20 years after the speech I had made in June 1951 urging this course (see Appendix I).

To mention reform of the Church in the same breath as reform of the limited liability company may seem bizarre. But there is a connection. Fellowship both in worship and work is the way to social and moral progress. After the war of 1939-45 the structures of both church and company were in need of reform. In both institutions the problem was, and is, to establish a basis of common purpose within an agreed moral objective. The change in the constitution of the Church of England had taken 50 years to bring about. The reform of Company law looks like taking even longer. In an effort to accelerate the process I made up my mind in 1985 to try once more to state the case for re-casting company law. The result was *The Just Enterprise*, published by André Deutsch in 1987.

CHAPTER XXXIV

Lectures & Sermons

From 1950 onwards for twenty years, I was doing a great deal of speaking on a variety of subjects. The Laity Challenge Fund meant addressing dozens of meetings of the lay people of Oxfordshire and its neighbouring counties Berkshire and Buckinghamshire, which together accounted for 620 parishes. Then there were 43 diocesan conferences of which I must have addressed a third. Then there were speeches to be made in the Church Assembly on among other things the poverty of the clergy, the rights of the laity, synodical government, church state relations, canon law revision, gambling, the church in industry, the moral law, and the *New English Bible*.

I preached the University sermon in St Giles Cathedral, Edinburgh on 29 April 1962 before the City fathers and University professors. As I made to climb into the high pulpit I suddenly realised that having no degree I was not entitled to wear an academic gown and said so to the Beadle. He replied as he robed me: 'Ye'l no go into John Knox's pulpit without a goon', which fateful words I found steadying rather than the reverse.

On another occasion, this time at the University Church, Oxford, I found myself preaching on 'Church reform true and false', from the very same pulpit whence Thomas Cranmer had made his final plea before being burnt to death.

The Authors' Association asked me to address them on the subject of Censorship and Licence. In the course of my talk I said 'there must be a certain congruity between the outer (collective) and inner (individual) order, lest by destroying the outward forms of morality through denial we take away man's inner freedom. There is no longer anything to revolt from'.

This emphasis on the moral order found its way into almost everything I said or wrote, and still does.

Some of the speeches and sermons are listed below :

October 1937
Christian Frontier Council, 'Problems of the Special Areas'

October 1941
Association for Planning & Regional Reconstruction, 'Ends and Means in Planning'

May 1944
All Souls Group on Education, 'The Rise of the Welfare State'

September 1945
Christian Frontier Council, 'Usury Then and Now'

May 1947
Trinity College, Cambridge, 'Ideals and Business'

January 1948
Oxford University Christian Socialists, 'Problems of Economic Responsibility'

January 1950
William Temple Society, Cambridge, 'Human Relations in Industry'

May 1952
BBC, 'To Whom in is Industry Responsible'

February 1953
Institute of Personnel Administration, 'Concept of Total Cooperation'

February 1953
Bath & Wells Diocesan Conference, 'Church and State'

June 1953
Liverpool Diocesan Conference, 'Church and State'

June 1953
Norwich Diocesan Conference, 'Church and State'

November 1953
King's College London, 'Social & Economic Conditions in Palestine in Year One'

December 1953
BBC, 'The Ethics of Gambling'

December 1953
Industrial Welfare Society, 'A Philosophy for Enterprise'

March 1954
Institute for Personnel Management, 'A Philosophy for Enterprise'

June 1954
Lawyers' Christian Fellowship, 'Church and State'

August 1954
Church Assembly, 'Report on Evanston'

June 1955
Evangelical Fellowship, 'Justice and Industry'

November 1955
Industrial Welfare Society, 'Human Implication of Management's Responsibilities'

December 1956
National Coal Board, 'Towards a Philosophy of Enterprise'

November 1957
Church Assembly, 'The Law and the Gospel'

June 1958
British Institute of Management, 'The Director's Role'

November 1958
Shell Mex & BP, 'Industry's Social Responsibility'

October 1959
British Institute of Management, 'The Responsibility of Industry to the Community'

February 1962
Authors' Association, 'Censorship and Licence'

April 1962
University Sermon, Edinburgh, 'Authority, Liberty and Participation'

October 1962
Leeds Chamber of Commerce, 'Management's Responsibility'

January 1964
British Institute of Management, 'Responsibility of Industry'

February 1964
Exeter College, Oxford, 'The Right Use of Money'

November 1965
Oxford University Church, 'Church Reform: True and False Objectives'

November 1969
Oxford Art Society, 'Can Art survive Industrialism?'

January 1970
Rugby School, 'Conflict and Grace'

May 1976
The Industrial Society, 'The Responsible Company'

June 1980
British North American Committee, 'Natural Law and International Investment'

CHAPTER XXXV

The Art of Collecting*

What is the reason for the great increase of interest in collecting of all kinds? There is of course the financial aspect. In a time of rapid inflation there is good sense in putting at least some of one's money into objects of real value. But an object of value is only a hedge against inflation on two conditions, first that one is willing to sell it when the time comes and second that someone else is willing to buy it. The buying and selling of antiques, books and other objects of value is a tricky business. One is not likely to succeed in beating inflation unless one's knowledge is at least as great as that of the dealer who handles the sale. Moreover fashion changes, and the person who buys as a hedge against inflation is likely to be somewhat sensitive to the claims of fashion and will suffer when fashion changes. On the whole I think the safest rule for collecting is to fall in love whenever possible. We should collect because we are in love. If we collect for love, whether it be for love of beauty, for love of enlightenment or for love of history, we shall not make a mistake. Love has the strange quality of attracting the object of desire. The passion of the true collector is like a magnet; it brings into his or her ken the desired object with what to some seems like fatality and to others the work of guardian angels – I was once told that I have two guardian angels. One of them, I am sure, is a bibliophile. 25 years ago I found a copy of Erasmus *On the Creed* 1533 dedicated to the Earl of Wiltshire, Anne Boleyn's father with whom Cranmer had been sent on an Embassy to the Emperor about the marriage. Maggs wanted 100 guineas for this rare work and I could only afford 50. That was on a Friday afternoon. On the following Monday morning I happened to be in Francis Edwards' bookshop in the Marylebone High Street and my hand went straight to a copy of the 1637 *Book*

*Written for the Oxford Art Society, 25 November 1969

of Common Prayer – the one that caused Jenny Geddes to throw her stool at the preacher. It had the two rare leaves of prayers at the end which are usually missing and it was on large paper. I bought it for £1 and took it round to Maggs and asked Mr Ernest Maggs if he had ever seen a large copy before with the two leaves of missing prayers. 'Yes, once,' he said. How much did you sell it for? £150 he said. So I handed him my copy and he let me take away the Erasmus in exchange. Accident or design? I could give many such examples. 'All mankind loves a lover' says Emerson, and it certainly applies to the collector who loves books. As in everything else you get out what you put in. There is a conspiracy in nature to help the man who really wants something, to get what he wants.

Is it too late to start a collection that is likely to be (a) interesting (b) comprehensive (c) educative and (d) worthwhile? Yes if you follow the fashion and collect French impressionists and Turner drawings or Constable oil sketches. Luckily most of us are not millionaires and are not interested in fashionable things. I am amazed when I look around at the opportunities still lying open to collectors. Two of the greatest Englishmen of the 19th century are John Ruskin and William Morris. They are both men of destiny. One was the greatest art critic of his time, wrote possibly the most influential English book of the century, and a splendid autobiography. The other was the reviver of the crafts, a poet and a founder of the socialist movement.

Both Morris and Ruskin wrote fine prose and thought great thoughts. Their books can be acquired in original condition for a few pounds each. They are a treasury of history, art, politics and wisdom. Again I have often wondered why no one seems to have thought of collecting humorous books. There is no better way of seeing the foibles of an age than through its humour, no quicker way of penetrating the spirit of a time. Like all collecting, it is an advantage to have started young. But in this respect the word young means what it means in the proverb 'He whom the Gods love dies young' which means, of course, he whom the gods love die *feeling young*. It is an advantage to have discovered what one really wants to do in collecting as in life before one is 30. Then one may with luck have 40 years or so in which to find what one wants – and that is not a day too long in order to find it. 'All things come to him who knows how to wait' but one has to keep alert and know what one is looking for.

What can collecting do for one? It can illuminate hidden corners of history, of language, of place.

Take history. I have always thought Anne Boleyn has been misjudged and that the reason she was beheaded was political. She was a reformer and sheltered and befriended reformers at the Court. If you were to collect all the books which contain on their title pages the Royal Arms impaling those of Anne Boleyn which were issued during her short reign of barely three years (1533-36) you would find they add up to powerful plea for her innocence and virtue. That she was at the centre of the movement of religious reform in these three years is clear from the books themselves, their authors and subjects. If you were to collect the books published by William Marshall who was a distinguished lawyer and friend of the Queen's you would find the titles in s t c (the *Short Title Catalogue of English Books published before 1640*) include Erasmus' *Treatise on the Creed* which I referred to a minute ago and which he dedicated to the Earl of Wiltshire, Anne's father, and Marsilius of Padua's *Defence of Peace* which is one of the earliest of the books advocating what we call democracy – the right of the people to participate in the decisions, political and religious, which affect them. Never again after Anne's death, was Henry to lend his authority to such democratic, not to say subversive, publications. From the mere study of these books one can learn something fresh about history.

How can we readily form a judgment for ourselves on the much discussed subject of who wrote the plays of Shakespeare – Bacon or Southampton or another? The answer is look at the preliminary pages of any of the folios. The answer is given in the preliminary leaves. Two of the actors who acted with Shakespeare, Henry Condell and John Heming, were responsible for their collection and publication after Shakespeare's death. The book is its own certificate of authorship. No one but Shakespeare can be the author – or J. Heminge and H. Condell were dissimulating villains and not plain actors. Their simple and straightforward preface shows they were the latter beyond any reasonable doubt. Study of the books themselves drives away false opinions.

I said one could find hidden corners of language as well as history. Some years ago I was studying a copy of Christopher St Germain's *Doctor and Student*. He by the way was another friend of Anne Boleyn's. St Germain was a lawyer who wrote the most influential law treatise of the 16th century. It was the standard work on the principles of English law until Blackstone's *Commentaries* and went through over 20 editions. I came upon a section which talked of sinderesis. This is a word which has been completely abandoned and there is no modern equivalent in the English language. Let me read you the passage:

'Sinderesis is a natural power of the soul set in the highest power thereof moving and stirring it to good and abhorring evil. And therefor sinderesis never sins or errs. And this sinderesis our Lord put in man to the intent that the order of things should be observed...

Sinderesis is more than conscience. It is the apprehension of order in the universe; the apprehension of a unity in the nature of things... Sinderesis is the beginning of all things that may be learned by speculation or study... And also of all things that are to be done by man.'

This is not merely an interesting bit of legal history. It is also a clue to what has gone wrong in Church and State in our generation.

I said that collecting and studying books can illuminate hidden corners of history, language and place. I have given examples in history and language. As to place I know a friend who lives in an old rectory not far from here. He is interested in collecting books connected with Oxford. Amongst these is an Oxford printer who published in the early 1600s. To his surprise and delight my friend found that the printer was the son of an Oxford parson who lived in the very house in which he was living and the Oxford printer had been born in the same house as his own children!

I want now to go on to the question of relating collecting to life. Why do we collect works of art and why does collecting mean so much to us in these days? I think it is partly a desire for continuity. The sense of continuity is strong in the English and it must find some outlet. Gardening doesn't quite satisfy our need for historical continuity, spiders' webs of new roads underfoot, the roar of aeroplanes overhead and the tearing down of old buildings around us give us an itch to try and save something from the general wreck, hence our desire to collect. A collection which covers a long period helps us to get a perspective. It enables us to put the present aside for a while so that we can return to it with a fresh mind.

Our aesthetic needs are another reason for collecting.

Dr Johnson's description of poetry as 'the art of uniting pleasure with truth by calling imagination to the help of reason' is true of the arts generally, and is a good summary of the function of art in life. All true and good art unites pleasure with truth, and does so by calling upon the imagination to illuminate reason. Reason by itself is a prison. It cannot escape from its own bounds. We need the faculty of imagination to take us beyond reasoning to what lies behind it. We may call it intuition, the knowledge of the heart – or faith, the knowledge of the soul. 'Imagination is a representation of what eternally exists, really and unchangeably.' 'The oak dies as well as the lettuce, but its eternal image and individuality never dies, but renews by its seed; just so the imaginative image returns by the seed of contemplation. This world of imagination is the world of eternity.' (W. Blake in his *Descriptive Catalogue*.) Or we can say that art is emotional experience transmitted by form; whether it be through a piece of music, sculpture, painting or poem.

The scientific revolution in which we live with its emphasis on fact and machinery, has made it hard for us to exercise our imaginations to discover the truth behind the facts, to apprehend the meaning of incommensurables like faith and love, and thus to reconcile the contraries. Plato's belief in an ideal and permanent idea behind the flux of reality – the idea of an oak that keeps the oak faithful to itself – is less easy for us moderns to grasp than Aristotle's view that there are no ideas or ideals behind reality apart from the reality itself. In religion we see the Church losing its agelong belief in an ideal of justice ordained by God Himself 'the law of the Lord is an undefiled law converting the soul' (Psalm 19). As a result of this loss of vision or imagination we are the poorer. For as Emil Brunner says 'the best possible system can only be created where the truly just has not been lost sight of.' So the degree of justice we can aim at, in the laws of industry or marriage or in the protection of human life, is limited and reduced by the failure of our vision, our inability to imagine a different and better order of things.

All this leads us to place upon art a weight which it can scarcely bear unaided by religion. To a certain extent we are trying to make art do the work of religion in opening up the vision of a better world where truth and justice flourish, where reason and emotion walk hand in hand with truth.

Work is the main activity of our lives and it is our work that gives us significance in the eyes of our fellowmen and women. I often wonder if the mania for collecting works of art is not connected with the separation of art from work in our daily lives, especially in the lives of the factory worker and commercial salesman. John Ruskin defined art in 1857 as 'that particular branch of human labour which is concerned not with the procuring of food but with the expression of emotion'. (*Political Economy of Art*, page 28.)

And William Morris in 1880 echoed this view when he said 'from the first dawn of history until quite modern times, art, which nature meant to solace all, fulfilled its purpose; all men shared in it, that was what made life romantic as people call it in these days, that and not robber barons and kings.'

The Bridge

The following nine chapters are written by Rosemary and provide a backcloth to the ideas and actions described in the first part of this book.

CHAPTER XXXVI

From North to South

My home in childhood was Rock Moor, an enlarged farmhouse four miles from the Northumbrian coast. The family name, Bosanquet, is French. All the Bosanquets in England are descended from one David Bosanquet, who left France in 1688, because of the persecution of the Protestants, known as Huguenots. His great-grandson, Charles, took over Rock Hall and the estate of five farms, from his wife's family, the Holfords, and my father was Charles' great-grandson. His name was Robert Carr Bosanquet. My mother was Ellen (usually called Nelly) Hodgkin, and was brought up near Newcastle-upon-Tyne, where my Quaker grandfather was a partner in a bank later engulfed by Lloyds. He also found time to write history. He married a cousin, Lucy Fox, from Falmouth. After my mother left Somerville College, Oxford, where she read History, she went on to study painting at the Slade.

My father specialised in Classics at Eton and Cambridge and made such a reputation for himself as a humorist, that he was invited to join the staff of *Punch*. Instead, he became an archaeologist, and by the time he married was Director of the British School at Athens. My eldest brother Charles was born there, but Violet, Diana, Lucy and David were born in Liverpool, when he had become Professor of Classical Archaeology at the University there. I was the only one of the family to be born at Rock Moor, which became our family home after my grandfather's death. During my youth Rock Hall was occupied by tenants, and from 1939 to 1945 by the Army. It then became a Youth Hostel, but is now back in family hands, as a school.

Before I was born, in 1918, my parents realised that they had failed to name any of their children after the most distinguished member of the family, my father's uncle, the philosopher Bernard

Bosanquet, so I was given Bernard for a second name even though I was not the boy they hoped for. I was called by my first name, Rosemary, until I was five, when I remember my father saying that in future I would be called Roma. To my family and school-friends I have been Roma ever since, but when I went up to Oxford I decided to use my original name.

Rock Moor is an ideal place for children, with its large garden, and the moors and the coast only a short drive away. David was only 18 months older, and allowed me to share in most of his activities, until he went away to boarding school at the age of nine. The only cloud over our happiness was the unpredictable nature of our father's temper. Sudden scolding was like a storm coming out of a clear sky. I realise now that many factors combined to make his life difficult. The Twenties were a time of agricultural depression, but he refused to dismiss any workers. He took on all the local responsibilities expected of a land-owner, which meant many committee meetings, and still worked as an archaeologist, being responsible for the excavation of Housesteads, one of the forts on the Roman Wall. There always seemed to be some letter or article that he was struggling to finish. The roast would be ready, or the car at the door, and we would all be waiting.

If my children have found me pernickety about punctuality, it is due to these memories of one person's lateness upsetting a whole household. The feeling of never quite catching up with all he wanted to do may have been one cause of my father's shortness of temper. He had been seriously ill with malaria in Greece and suffered occasional recurrences. To look back to his own child-hood, he had five older sisters and one younger, who perhaps spoiled him, and thereby made my mother's position difficult later on.

My mother's Quaker background, strong personal faith and genuine love for my father, stood her in good stead and often enabled her to shield their children from his irritability. She had a wry sense of humour that surfaced at unexpected moments. Although remaining a member of the Society of Friends, she ran the local Sunday School, and brought us to church once a week.

She managed to write and have published two books about Athens, in spite of domestic interruptions.

After David went to boarding school, I continued to have lessons, sometimes at home, sometimes staying in other families, sharing their governesses, not very happy experiences. In the middle of one summer term the doctor suggested that drinking the water at a French Spa would improve my father's health, and as David had found his prep school unhealthy, it was decided that he and I should go with our parents, a wholly happy interlude, and our first taste of 'abroad'. The only book provided for holiday reading was *Don Quixote*, and I read it all. I realised that French was a living language and struggled to speak it. That experience was helpful when I started at Hayes Court, the boarding-school in Kent where all my sisters had been, at the age of eleven. In 1987 I edited a book about Hayes Court called *Hayseed to Harvest*, so I will pass over my time there, only expressing my gratitude for teaching that enabled me to get a scholarship to Somerville at the age of 17.

George has described how he came in 1936 to Rock Moor for Christmas. From then on, letters linked us, and he came up to Oxford for several weekends. When he came to stay at Rock in April, my family realised that we were definitely committed to each other, and so did my close friends at Oxford after the start of term. At this time George wrote 'I want you to feel as free as possible, so that you will be able to roam (no pun intended) where and as you will this term and the coming ones, and learn all you can, and meet lots of people. I want to stand well back in the rear of the picture.'

Within a month that view of the next two years was to change completely. My mother would normally have been the first person to be told, but she was just then preoccupied with my eldest sister Violet, who was at Rock Moor for the birth of her second baby, so it was to my other married sister, Lucy, that I poured out my heart.

'This is probably my last term at Oxford; you see George and I quite definitely want to get married in September or October.

Only I don't feel this is quite the moment to consult the family, with Vi's baby holding up all the plans for the summer, and Diana (my other sister) about to get married any day... so you needn't mention it to anyone just yet. At least, I expect everybody knows, they always do know everything before one knows oneself. What nobody knows is that we've bought a house. We didn't mean to, but we came on it by accident on Whit-Sunday, and it was so perfect, and just what we wanted, that we bought it on Whit-Monday, just like that. It really is absolutely heavenly, in a Chiltern village called Kidmore End, near enough to Reading for G to get to London in an hour, 16th Century (with all modern conveniences) and Cromwell stabled his horses there, I can't think why, so it's called Cromwell Cottage. We have now owned it for nearly a month, and as yet no snags have appeared. Since then we've been furnishing it, and my mind has been torn between the 100 Years War, and whether to buy that secondhand Hoover. And life is quite ridiculous, and very good, and I'm not quite as mad as I sound, only rather happy... we obviously can't go on like this for two years, and if I'm not going to finish here I might as well go down now and give my place to some 'poor girl' whom the college can be proud of.'

I rambled on like this for two more pages. I had quite forgotten writing this letter until one of Lucy's daughters sent it to me after her death more than 50 years later. I wish I could thank her for having kept it so long! As she had married within a year of leaving Somerville she could understand my feelings.

Why were we so sure on that sunny Whit-Sunday in 1937 that Cromwell Cottage was meant to be our home? George has mentioned that we spent the day of King George VI's Coronation together, earlier that week. Then we explored the Chiltern beechwoods in their May glory, and I saw bluebells for the first time. Over lunch in the Swan at Streatley, George borrowed a railway time-table and said 'We could live near here and I could get to London every day'. When he came up to Oxford the next weekend, spending the night at the Eagle and Child pub in St Giles, we had no intention of exploring the Chilterns again. We were due to spend Sunday with his parents at Walton-on-Thames, and meant to drive straight there. But we began the day with 8 o'clock Communion at St Mary's, the University Church, and from then on the signposts were all signs of Grace. We drove to Wallingford, where we had breakfast at the George Hotel. Why there? Why not in Oxford? We sat at a table with a couple who were enthusiastic about Mapledurham, which they had visited the day before. It seemed a small diversion from our route, so we set off, took a wrong turning in the Chiltern lanes, and found ourselves at Kidmore End, staring at the For Sale sign in the garden of Cromwell Cottage. It had only been put up the day before.

The owner was at church across the road, but her companion-help showed us over the house. Feeling that we were intended by providence to buy it, we agreed to come back the next day, Whit-Monday, to negotiate. George had saved enough from his salary for us to be able to buy it outright, and still afford to furnish it. From then on my term was disrupted by telegrams saying 'Meet me at Sotheby's (or Christie's) to-morrow.' At the time of his previous engagement, he had got to know a Cockney furniture restorer and marquetry cutter called Albert Dunn, who regularly scoured the salerooms for him, and fully understood what we needed for a sixteenth-century cottage with two larger modern rooms added on.

We soon realised that this house was not going to be left empty, or inhabited by George alone for the next two years. To-day the position would be different, but married students were unheard of before the War. My mother, an old Somervillian herself, was philosophical when we told her our plans. Two of my sisters, Diana and Lucy, had followed in her footsteps, and stayed the course.

George came up to Rock Moor for my 19th birthday in July, and we discussed plans for a wedding on 18 September. We walked on the moors, and swam in the sea, and he seemed fit and well. Yet within a short time after he returned to the south he became desperately ill, as he described in Chapter XIII. After a few days of anxiety, I went up to London to be near him, staying with one of my six maiden-aunts, my father's sisters. Aunt Bessie lived in St John's Wood, and was a great moral support. I travelled by train to Reading, and the builder who was renovating the cottage met me in his car. George had intended to supervise the work, but was now feeling too weak even to talk about that, or about any wedding arrangements. However, I did go to Felix Weiss' studio, and had several sittings for the bust which he had promised as a wedding present, and which George refers to in Chapter XIV. When George was feeling stronger, a new date was fixed for the wedding. 5 November! I realised when I returned to Rock that I must find something to do for the next three months, preferably well away from Somerville. Family contacts took me to West Cumberland, one of the districts worst hit by the Depression, designated a 'Special Area'. In the 'Special Areas' there was no employment at all. They had originally been called 'Depressed Areas' until it was realised that a less hopeless name would be more helpful, so 'Special Areas' they were, with a Commission, in charge of them, which provided work for some bureaucrats if few other people. One of the few was my first cousin Thomas Hodgkin, two years down from Oxford already and in the area, giving lectures to the unemployed. My brother David, in his vacation from Trinity, Cambridge, was further south, helping with a work-camp at Barrow-in-Furness. When he finished there it was arranged that he would leave behind the small Ford car he had been using, on which he and I had both learnt to drive, but which in our absence was no longer needed at Rock Moor. With this, I could be of use, as a driver to Gertrude Hodges, whom the Commission were paying to lecture about drama and encourage the unemployed, mostly iron and steel workers, to put on plays.

I enjoyed getting to know a new part of England, and helping with the practical side of preparing for plays in Village Halls and Clubs. Whether this helped to relieve the depression of the area is doubtful, but it certainly helped to relieve my depression. On my first evening Gertrude Hodges, whose digs in Whitehaven I was sharing, explained the complications of her job, bedevilled by dissension between the Cumberland Drama League, the National Council for Social Service, and the County Education Authority, as well as the Special Areas commission.

Gertrude came by train with me down to Barrow-in-Furness to collect the car. I had a hair-raising drive back over Hardknott Pass, then an unmetalled road, with many hairpin bends. At the top we stopped and spoke to a carload of people who had come up the other side, and urged us not to go down there as it was terribly dangerous. But we did and found it less nerve-wracking than the road we had come up. After that I was prepared to tackle any Cumbrian road.

Besides driving Gertrude to the scattered villages and mining towns, I was able to help Tommy Hodgkin get to the lectures he gave on such subjects as Psychology. I enjoyed hearing these, and as he had recently become engaged to a young Somerville don, we were mutually sympathetic. In future years Dorothy Crowfoot would make the name of Hodgkin internationally famous, gaining the O.M. and a Nobel prize for her work in crystallography.

I wrote to George almost every day, and quote from a typical letter. 'The job in hand at the moment is getting together men and women to go to a drama course, and the chief complication is of course the Dole. One woman said to me "We only get 26 shillings a week, and if I take my share out there won't be enough for the rent." So we dash to and fro, from village to village, trying to persuade people who can go, to do so.

It's incredibly lovely country here. The towns are depressing, but as soon as you get out you are on high ground, overlooking the slag-heaps and pit-chimneys.'

We did get enough people together for the drama course, and I helped ferry them for a weekend in Newlands, a beautiful unspoilt valley, where a professional actor produced the Fifth Act of *Twelfth Night*. Not many women had managed to leave their families, so I was given the part of Olivia.

I was able to get away for another weekend to stay with my sister Lucy. Michael Gresford-Jones her husband and first-cousin, was then Vicar at South Shore, Blackpool. It meant a very cross-country journey by train, but was well worthwhile, as George was able to come up from London and for the first time met Lucy and Michael. I think he combined business with pleasure, and visited a customer in Leeds on the way. His company supplied newsprint to newspaper publishers in many parts of the British Isles, and in later years many of our journeys included a call at a newspaper office. The business part of our Blackpool visit was discussing details of our wedding with Michael, who was to officiate in Rock church, with his father, my uncle Herbert the Bishop of Warrington, to preach the sermon. I had several weeks at home before that occasion, making happy preparations.

A few days before the wedding, there was an exciting party for friends and relations who lived in the south. Crosby Hall, on the site of Thomas More's home in Chelsea, was filled with a great mixture of people, from my elderly aunts to my ex-boyfriends. George's girlfriends sang and played stringed instruments, and we each met for the first time friends of the other who would continue to be our friends for years.

When George and his parents and brother Claude travelled north, they stayed at Rock Hall with Helen Sutherland, my family's very special tenant and friend. My brother David had forecast gloomily that a November wedding in Northumberland would result in 'flu for all, but the sun shone and we were photographed in the garden at Rock Moor, just as if it had been summer. Then we were driven to Newcastle, caught the train and began our new life together.

CHAPTER XXXVII

Pre-War & War-time

A month before Christmas we settled in at Cromwell Cottage. We had plenty of help during our early years there. The part-time gardener and his wife who had worked for our predecessor lived next door but one; King was tall and dark and laconic, but his wife was little and scurried about her work like Beatrix Potter's Mrs Tiggy-winkle. She kept the house beautifully clean, in an hour a day. They persuaded us also to employ their teenage daughter Kathy, who had not long left school, but who could cook and dish up a meal much more efficiently than I could, in spite of fancy cooking lessons at school and in Brussels, where I spent one term before going up to Oxford. My sisters Violet and Lucy had both begun their married lives with a maid, and we took it for granted that we would do the same.

It was also taken for granted that I would be called on by the neighbours, and would pay calls in return. I still have one specimen of the calling-card printed for that purpose. At the age of 19 I found it hard to take this procedure seriously. But it was not a total waste of time, for in at least two cases it led to friendships which have been revived by the next generation.

My mother and brother David came to spend Christmas with us. When I told my mother that I was already pregnant she lost no time in booking me a Maternity Nurse for the following August, the invaluable Scottie, who was even then seeing my sister Lucy's second daughter into the world. Before the baby was due, we replaced the Renault two-seater with a Vauxhall 4 door open coupé, which served us valiantly for 15 years. When the spring came we began gardening in earnest. The previous owner of the house was a keen gardener, and was still in the neighbourhood, so we did our best not to let her down. Mr King was only interested in the vegetables, and in mowing the lawn, and looked on rather sardonically at our efforts.

I think the best present I have ever had was and is my life-membership of the London Library, which George gave me about this time. His office was only ten minutes walk away, and when I did not come up to London he carried heavy loads of books home, though he never had to bring the generous allowance of 16 books all at once. I was able to follow up many different subjects during these months as a lady of leisure.

The leisure came to an end in August, when Daniel was born. After Christmas George began to hanker for a ski-ing holiday, so we engaged a temporary nanny to look after the baby at Rock Moor while we went away for two weeks. It was my first ski-ing holiday and the only one we had before the war. It would be more than ten years before we went ski-ing again, and I never recovered that first fine careless rapture. We also visited Zurich and I met his Swiss grandmother and other relatives.

The belief that war was on the way had been a factor in our decision to get married and establish a home and family before the storm broke. During 1938 the storm-clouds were building up ominously, and in September we all thought the time had come. The precautions being taken then seemed primitive, and it was a relief when Chamberlain bought off Hitler at Munich, to give a year's respite, but we realised that war had to come. I had seen the Nazis' bullying parades and marches when I had spent half-a-term at a German school on Lake Constance in 1933, and shared the apprehension of the Jewish pupils. Many girls from refugee families came to my school, Hayes Court, during the following years; after Austria was overrun my mother took in a husband and wife until they could get a passage to the U.S.A.

In July 1939 we put our apprehensions aside, and celebrated my 21st birthday with a weekend house-party, (though some guests had to sleep in tents in the orchard). This coincided with the Finals of Henley Regatta. We hired a punt from which to watch the races, but I enjoyed even more going to the Fair in the evening. I had managed to reach the age of 21 without ever going to a Fair, and riding on the Roundabout with George was the peak of my celebration.

The following weeks were overshadowed by war preparations, but brightened by news that employment was increasing even in the Special Areas. Air-raid precautions included the issue of gas masks to all. For babies, including Dan, there was a kind of sealable carry-cot, and for toddlers the gas masks were made as like as possible to Mickey Mouse, and brightly coloured.

CHAPTER XXXVIII

War-time

On Sunday 3 September the the smell of Sunday dinner cooking was the background to Chamberlain's radio speech saying that we were at war with Germany. Children were already being evacuated from London and other big cities, and Kidmore End's Women's Voluntary Services allocated Ronnie and Cyril Green to us. Aged 9 and 7, their behaviour caused no problems. But they both had a skin disease, impetigo, which one-year-old Dan soon caught. It could be cured by a Gentian-violet salve. Soon most of the village children had purple patches on their faces.

The time between September 1939 and May 1940 had a feeling of unreality; it was the 'phoney war', with troops in France waiting for something to happen. Rationing began gradually, and we all discussed the ethics of buying while supplies were still freely available. My mother's worst memory of 1914-18 shortages was having to use newspaper instead of toilet paper so she stockpiled that at Rock Moor. George bought model railways, gauge O, including perfect continental coaches like those in which we had travelled to Switzerland the previous spring. Before long it was forbidden to sell any toy costing more than £5. He also bought himself some clothes, including a green tweed suit; this he continued to wear during very cold weather until it was given to Oxfam in response to an appeal for warm clothes for Yugoslavian refugees 50 years later in 1992. The fact that he kept it so long is a credit to his figure as well as to the quality of the cloth.

My only extravagance was to buy a whole tin of mixed biscuits before they disappeared from the shops. After a few months plain biscuits were the only ones sold; one took a paper bag to put them in, and in return surrendered 'points' from the ration book, coupons which could be exchanged for a variety of items extra to the basic rations of meat, cheese and fats; later on bread was added. We had no idea that rationing would go on until 1954, long past the end of the war. We never suffered hardship from food-rationing, though other people did. The rations for children, including babies, and pregnant mothers were generous and throughout the war our household qualified on all counts.

After a few weeks Michael and Louise Bruce and their toddler daughter Mary came to visit us. Michael had been a friend of George's for some time and we found him and his Dutch wife very congenial. They had given up their London flat on the outbreak of war and were staying with elderly relatives three miles away, but the arrangement was becoming a strain, and could not be prolonged. We made inquiries, and found that Ronnie and Cyril would be welcome at another house in Kidmore End; when they left us the Bruces moved in.

Michael Bruce was the Secretary of the National Fitness Council, an organisation hastily set up by the government when they realised how unhealthy the nation was becoming. This Council's main purpose was to increase the amount of exercise taken by everyone. Was it with this in mind that George challenged Michael one weekend to a really long walk over the Berkshire Downs? Early in the morning they set off from Streatley up onto the Icknield Way and on to Avebury where Louise and I met them with a car in the evening. George claimed that he was less exhausted than Michael.

When petrol rationing started, George was allowed enough coupons to go to Reading station and back as well as the basic ration allowed to all car owners at first. When the newsprint stocks were dispersed to country locations (see p.64) he was allocated extra petrol to enable him to make spot checks on these sites and the condition of the rolls. With a map and much ingenuity this enabled us to have days off, he from the office, and I from the family, and explore unknown areas of country. There was no need to use the car for shopping. The village post office, five minutes away, kept all essential groceries. Sonning Common, half an hour's walk with a pram, or ten minutes on a bicycle, had several other shops and a half hourly bus service to Reading.

A smaller bus to Reading actually passed the house twice a day.

There was a bitterly cold spell in the early months of 1940, and in spite of the efforts of Mr King, our small vegetable patch was soon bare. I vividly remember going to Sonning Common and coming back in triumph with one swede for supper. I would never be so conscious of food shortages again. This was due to our nearness to the Vicarage, and its large walled garden with a glebe orchard between us and the church.

Soon after we arrived in Kidmore End, George was asked to become Churchwarden. The Vicar at that time was a widower, Mr Bird. He had one son, who came and went, and we realised that the Vicar was an unhappy man, but never managed to get to know him. One evening soon after the outbreak of war George was sent for; Mr Bird was sitting with a loaded shotgun and the question was whether he intended to use it on himself or on someone else. George sat there for over an hour, in the company of an intrepid ex-missionary, Miss Gunston, until Mr Bird's son arrived with a doctor and an ambulance and he was taken away, to die naturally a few weeks later. His successor at the Vicarage was a bachelor, and soon asked us if we would like to take over the orchard and the walled garden, which included a fruit cage and an asparagus bed. From then on we had all the vegetables and fruit we could eat and some to give away. In the summer of 1940 as the phoney war became a real war, and country after country succumbed to German troops, I could get up early in the morning, collect vegetables, and pick fruit, to be dealt with later in the day. This continued to be my solace throughout the war years.

Kathy King was soon called up into the Forces, but her young sister Dora, straight from school at the age of 15, was a much better hand at cooking a Sunday lunch than I was. The early summer of 1940 was a desperately worrying time for the King family, as their only son's regiment had been engulfed by the German invasion, and there was no news of him for many weeks after the fall of France. Each fine morning the post van would arrive; letters for us, nothing for the Kings. Their anxiety was all the greater because the boy had left school without learning to read or write. To-day he would have been diagnosed as dyslexic. At last a Red Cross postcard announced that he was a prisoner of war, but they had no other communication until he came home in 1944.

After the fall of France, when it seemed probable that England would be invaded, we faced the reality of war. Air-raid precautions and the strict blackout of windows and car headlights (except for a narrow slit) now seemed vital, instead of merely irritating. The Great Western Railway ran normally and even in the blackout George could reach home from Reading station in half an hour. He often brought friends with him especially after the bombing of London began; they were glad to come to the country for a quiet night. The Bruce family had moved on, so we had a guest room, even after the birth of Ellen in early October. My brother Charles was staying with us that weekend, and we were all busy picking apples in the garden and orchard, when I became aware of her imminent and unexpectedly early arrival. The District Nurse and our local GP helped her into the world, as our friend Scottie, who had seen me through Dan's birth, had not yet come.

The victory in the air, the Battle of Britain, had cheered us all in the previous weeks, and we were feeling confident that we would not now share the fate of France. Bombing raids on London and other cities intensified, but George still managed to get home for the night, except when on 'Firewatching' duty in his office. Then he could sleep on a camp bed until a raid started, when sand buckets and shovels were prepared for action against incendiary bombs and he stood on the roof expecting the worst. Against high-explosive bombs no precautions could be taken. Other buildings in Pall Mall, including the Carlton Club, received direct hits, but George's office and the Reform Club opposite stayed intact. After an uncomfortable night he could go across and eat breakfast in civilized surroundings, though the breakfast would be sparse in accordance with rationing. Even previously expensive restaurants were forbidden to charge more than five shillings (more than £5 today) for any meal.

The fact that George regularly had a midday meal that did not come out of our rations obviously helped us to have something to spare for overnight guests. Visitors who came for longer usually brought little offerings of butter and sugar, since ration books were registered with particular shops and could only be transferred with difficulty and attendance at the local 'Food Office'.

Many of our overnight visitors belonged to the Christian Frontier Council. Several others were connected with the Association for Planning and Regional Reconstruction, which George mentions in chapter XIV. Looking back, I find it remarkable that even in 1941 people were working on plans for peacetime. I was able to go with George to two of their weekend conferences, one at Llanthony Abbey in Monmouthshire, one in the Gower Peninsula, leaving the children at home. This interest in planning stood George in good stead a few years later, when he was co-opted to fill a vacancy on the Henley Rural District Council, and was able to persuade them that the Council houses being built after the war should be sited in groups, and not as ribbon development along the road.

After the birth of William, in May 1942, I stayed at home, but visitors still came, including elderly aunts and George's parents from Walton-on-Thames. My mother too continued to travel, visiting her scattered family. By now the basic petrol ration had been stopped, but buses and trains ran punctually, and the question 'Is your journey really necessary?' was not yet posed over every booking-office.

There was less bombing of London for a while, but we heard the German planes droning overhead at night, and wondered which historical city they aimed to destroy in retaliation for the R.A.F. raids on Germany. There was horrifying news from the Far East after Japan's entry into the war, but this was balanced by the knowledge that the United States was now an ally. Soon American friends in uniform were coming to stay, and the Supreme Allied Headquarters was established in St James's Square round the corner from George's office. We managed to go to Rock Moor for a holiday in the summer of 1943, and were there when the news came that Italy having been invaded by the Allies had capitulated. We hoped this would mean freedom for my sister Violet's husband. He did get away from his P.O.W. camp before the Germans took over, and hid with friendly peasants until he could make his way to Switzerland, where he had to stay till the end of the war. George sent him a message urging him to use his skis which had been left in the care of his cousin, and this he did.

We had a succession of different helpers, usually 'living-in', but there were days when I was quite alone with the children, and felt delighted to welcome the neighbour who came round to collect War Savings as someone to talk to.

In the next village, Cane End, the substantial Queen Anne House had been owned by an eccentric old squire, Mr Vandersteegen, who collected steam-rollers and traction engines. They were kept in a field near the road, and were a goal for walks with the pram. By 1941, the engines had all gone, probably to be salvaged and the iron re-used; the squire was dead, and the house was taken over by a private school from London, known as Miss Clutten's School. Only some of the pupils came with it as boarders, and local children were needed to fill up the places. Dan and Ellen started in the nursery class on reaching the age of three. This was an unexpected piece of good fortune, as nursery schools were unknown in country areas. The school was allowed petrol for collecting its day pupils, but its nearest pick-up point was a mile away. At first I took Dan there on a basket seat on the back of my bicycle, but when Ellen succeeded to that position, Dan whizzed along the road on his second-hand tricycle (nothing like that could be bought new) and parked it inside the gate of a friendly cottage. There was very little traffic, apart from tradesmen's vans and the twice-daily bus.

As well as collections for War Savings, there were constant appeals for gifts, in money and in kind, to help the war effort. The first came from Lord Beaverbrook, when he became Minister of Aircraft Production, asking housewives for aluminium saucepans, so that they could be turned into aeroplanes. We sacrificed some of ours; it was only years later that we learnt that in fact the country had plenty of aluminium, and the pans were not needed. But perhaps appealing to people and making them feel part of the aircraft industry was good for morale.

A railway journey to the north was always good for my morale. The Newsprint Supply Company commissioned the building of three ships to replace those lost through enemy action. When the first was completed, I was asked to launch her and christened her *Kelmscott*. There was a lunch after the launch, and although it was a celebration for the ship and her builders, our hearts were anxious for her crew. In fact the *Kelmscott*, and her sister ships the *Baskerville* and the *Caxton* both survived the war. The worst of the submarine attacks were now over.

My only practical contribution to the war effort was brief. Early one summer there was a shortage of digitalis, used for making heart medicine. The local W.V.S. asked if I could arrange the harvesting of fox-glove leaves, which provide digitalis, and which grew plentifully in some of the Chiltern beechwoods. I had one friend and ally nearby, Ailsa de Mille, who had children the same age as Ellen and William, and she helped to organise the local teenagers, who had been complaining that they had nothing to do. We led them to a clearing near Cane End and packed sacks full of leaves, which were then taken to the local mental hospital, dried in the boiler-room, and sent on to a pharmaceutical company. We never heard any more about this, but it did have one useful result. It led us to start the parish's first youth club, and run it, until a trained youth-leader was appointed to take over.

The Allied Forces invaded France in June 1944. We hoped that this as well as the freeing of the French people would lead to a cessation of the night bombing of London, which had been resumed during the previous winter. It did; but a worse menace was to come, in the shape of pilotless aircraft, 'V-1s', or 'Flying bombs', which crashed and exploded when the engine cut out. The south-east of England suffered as well as London, and the strain on all the inhabitants was increased because they might come at any hour of the day or night, so that the warning sirens went off constantly. The offices of the Allied High Command had a special warning signal when a V-1 was approaching towards it, and George learnt to identify this sound. When he heard it, he would continue work underneath his desk, not having gone down to the basement with the rest of the staff.

The 'V-2' rockets, which added to the horror that autumn, led to massive loss of life, but came silently out of the sky, without the nerve-wracking wait for the engine of the V-1 to cut out.

Our Visitors' Book lists many people who had re-settled back in London, and were glad to leave it for a quiet night or two, including my brother Charles, now rejoined by his wife Barbara, who had been in the United States with their children since before the start of the war. George's brother Cecil came back from Delhi, where he was Technical Director of All India Radio, having been responsible for setting up the network. Claude, the youngest of the three, was also an engineer, working for the Admiralty on the supply of optical glass for the Royal Navy.

There are no signatures in the Visitors' Book for October and November 1944, except that of Scottie who was with us for the birth of Lucy Jane. There are no entries for December, for after Scottie left, we had no help in the house at all, illness having removed the middle-aged woman who had been with us for some months. All young women were called up for service in the Forces or the Factories, equally vital; at least I thought this was so. George was more hopeful, and was led by Providence to the National Children's Home in Harpenden where he found Vera Orman, aged 18, newly qualified as a Nursery Nurse. She had been looking forward to the Christmas celebrations at the Home, but he persuaded her to come to us without any delay. We got on wonderfully well together, and when the time came for her to be called up, a tribunal decided that with four children to look after our household could be regarded as her form of war-work.

CHAPTER XXXIX

Moving On

Looking back, I wonder how we managed to go on putting up visitors in the now overcrowded Cromwell Cottage. Our guests in the spring of 1945 included George's American boss, Richard Doane, a large bachelor, used to his comforts. He had flown the Atlantic sitting in a bomb-rack, since there were as yet no commercial transatlantic flights; he probably regarded staying with us as another unavoidable war-time discomfort.

We were beginning to hope that the war was nearly over; encouraged by Winston Churchill's forecast that 1945 would bring peace not only in Europe but also in the Far East. For the first time in five years we felt able to look ahead. George had always thought of Cromwell Cottage as our home for life, but now he agreed that we would have to move. We went house-hunting, at first on our bicycles, and when the basic petrol ration was restored, by car. My memories of that spring are so full of house-hunting that I have no definite memory of the end of the war in Europe, partly because we had been expecting the news for days. VE Day, as it was called, was on the 8 May, and very soon afterwards came our own great day.

George came home with an estate agent's description that had been sent for some reason to his office. We were somewhat disillusioned with these descriptions by now, and this one actually managed to make the house sound unattractive, mentioning stucco. But it was in Rotherfield Greys, three miles away, a village that always attracted me when we drove across the Green on our way to Henley. Vera was out that evening, so George set out on his bicycle to have a preliminary look. He came back so excited that he could hardly speak, just saying 'Come! come!' I had to ask Mrs King to come in and babysit, and we set off, by car this time.

We had no appointment or order to view, but the Hungarian

domestics cheerfully showed us round, and before darkness fell we knew it was for us. Stucco? a little on the wall of the back premises; elsewhere there was old brick showing through a pink wash put on some years before.

The name 'Benfold Place' had no local connections, and disguised the fact that this was the Old Rectory, begun in the 16th century, added to in the 17th, and completed with a fine Georgian front, looking east down the valley towards Henley, west towards Greys Court, and with a huge sloping field opposite. Later we learnt that this was called Parson's Hill, but it was not included in the 12 acres that went with the house. What was included was a walled garden, a lawn big enough for unconventional football, cricket and croquet, a field with cowslips and wild daffodils and a beech wood. The path into the wood was almost choked by nettles and brambles, but we could see the bluebells beyond.

A deposit was paid the next day, before we had even met the owners, or viewed the house officially. It was a good thing we were so quick, because we learnt afterwards that the occupant of the Dower House at Greys Court coveted this house, in full view of his windows, but did not hear it was for sale until it was too late. We felt that once again the signs of grace had led us to make a quick decision.

We had to wait two months before moving in and it took most of that time to sell Cromwell Cottage. Before we had a firm offer George had to go to Canada to renew links with the colleagues whom he had not seen for seven years. In his absence I accepted a slightly lower price than we had agreed, but any house left empty was liable to be requisitioned to house the homeless; by losing some money we gained peace of mind.

George crossed the Atlantic on one of the Newsprint Supply Co. ships, taking ten days, but came back more swiftly by flying boat. The move from Cromwell Cottage followed immediately. The prospect of having room to expand overcame our regrets at leaving the house where we had been so happy for eight years.

We chose a name for our new home that did have a local connection. The beechwood was known in the village as Pinder's Wood, after a Rector who had lived in the house for 40 years. We decided to extend that name to the house with a spelling alteration in order to connect it also with the Greek poet.

We were happy to find that the full-time gardener was willing to go on working for us. Mr Woodcock was a stocky man with a beaming smile; he had lost his job as a steelworker in Sheffield during the Depression, and moved south to find work. He had no training as a gardener, but knew and loved this garden that was now ours. He was used to stoking the central heating boiler in the cellar, and brought up the anthracite with which we made up the Aga in the kitchen.

It was a great joy to me to have an Aga to cook on, a link with Rock Moor. The kitchen was large enough to hold a round table for family meals. There was also plenty of room in the back premises for a refrigerator and a washing machine. Very few people in England possessed either of these appliances, so we had not felt deprived at not having them at Cromwell Cottage. We took it for granted that though the sheets and bath-towels went to the laundry, all the other washing for ourselves and four children was done by hand, rinsed in the bath, put through a hand-turned wringer, and hung out in the orchard to dry if it was fine. All the babies' nappies had to be washed; disposable ones had not been invented.

The improvement in our life-style was even more obvious in the front of the house. At Cromwell Cottage the front-door had opened directly into the dining-room. Here there was a small porch, and beyond a door, a large hall, created out of two living rooms when the house ceased to be a Rectory. The Steinway grand piano fitted into part of the far end, leaving room for a sofa and armchairs in front of the fireplace, which devoured all the logs we could get from the wood, and only smoked when the wind came from a particular part of the east. The other part of the room had a built-in bookshelf along the outer wall, and two pillars near the Georgian staircase. The pillars concealed steel girders to support the upper storeys, since two internal walls had been removed. There was a parquet floor, and we left that end of the hall empty, so that the children could play there, and dance to George's accordion. Later on it was perfect for parties and even wedding receptions, though they did not come into our thoughts in 1945. There was a study for George with a bay window, and a big dining room near the kitchen. Upstairs there were three big bedrooms, a day nursery and a tiny bedroom, as well as three attic-rooms. The central heating did not extend to the latter, but our children slept in them without complaint; verbal complaints were absent, but of course there were plenty of the other kind; all the infectious diseases, at one time or another.

Most of these ailments were probably contracted at the Village School, ten minutes walk away on the Village Green. For the first term Dan and Ellen were there it was overcrowded; an elderly teacher coped with children up to the age of eleven. After that the older children were sent by bus to the next village, a younger school-mistress was appointed, and all our family had the first three years of their education there.

This helped us to feel part of the community, as did the discovery that the Rector, Robert Lloyd, was a distant cousin. He and his family had lived in our house until two years before the war and were a much more helpful source of information about it than our immediate predecessors. They also told us that Lady Brunner at Greys Court had a link with my mother's family, and that led to a friendship which has strengthened over the years. Her husband Sir Felix had Swiss ancestors, which made a bond with George.

The blissful first summer in our new home was only overshadowed by thoughts of people in other parts of the world still being oppressed by the Japanese. Even in Europe there was still starvation in many countries and rations in England were reduced so that more food could be sent to them. In August the horrifying news of the dropping of the Atomic bombs on Japan was quickly followed by VJ Day. Peace at last! after nearly six years of war.

George's daily routine stayed much the same. He had a longer drive to and from Reading station, but being able to use the car headlights made the drive easier in the winter. My life, however, was transformed by our new surroundings. I was soon involved in several local activities. The Village Hall was next to the school. If I was at an afternoon meeting the children could slip in after school and share in the tea.

During the winter, I was approached by some teenagers who asked if I would help them put on an entertainment in the Village Hall. The show was a success, and led to the suggestion a year later that the local drama group, which had been in abeyance during the war, should be revived. The expert, who had been their producer, had died, and after the first meeting I found myself committed to producing Shaw's *Arms and the Man*. It was an ambitious choice, but the cast required exactly fitted our few volunteers. They included Gerald Agnew, whose wife had recently died, so that he was glad on his return from Bond Street to come across from his home opposite the Village Hall, to join in rehearsals. Next to his house was the Forge, where Bill Barrett, the village blacksmith worked. Bill deserves a whole chapter to himself. He was church-warden, sexton, and a key-man in all aspects of parish life. But he made time to learn a part and rehearse. The longest part, that of the Swiss soldier of fortune, was taken by a young master at the local secondary school, who had come as a refugee from Germany just before the war. His strong foreign accent fitted in perfectly.

Several other plays followed, and drew in talent from other villages, including a much more experienced producer. I was glad to give up the responsibility, being engaged in productions of my own during the winter months. Giles was born in February 1947, and Hugh in November 1948.

Before those events I was able to make my first transatlantic trip. We were to leave in August 1946, and as our return would only be a short time after the beginning of term, decided to take Dan with us. His eighth birthday took place while we were on the Atlantic, on the maiden voyage of the *Baskerville*, which took us to Cornerbrook in Newfoundland. There was a Bowater paper-mill there, and very little else. It was an exciting place for a first land-fall in the New World.

We stayed in a hotel in Montreal for a few days, and I met many of George's friends and colleagues for the first time. Then we went down to New York by train. What astonished me there was not the buildings (I had seen pictures of skyscrapers) but the colours of the cars, and especially of the taxis, bright red and yellow, and all the colours of the rainbow. Only black cars had been manufactured in England during the war, and even before the war cars had mostly been dark-coloured. Our white Vauxhall was a striking exception. The heat in New York was oppressive, so I was glad when we went to stay with very old friends of George's, the Sebrings, near Philadelphia. Dan and I were with them for a week while George worked in New York. Then we all returned to Montreal. He had to fly back to England on one of the commercial flights that had just been started.

None of the Newsprint Supply Company's ships was due to cross the Atlantic just then, but passages for Dan and me were booked on an old Liberty ship called the *Sam Dell*, sailing from Montreal to Hull. We had stormier weather going back and this ship rolled much more than the *Baskerville*, in spite of being fully loaded, whereas the *Baskerville* had crossed in ballast. However, we neither of us felt sick. Dan, like all our family, was a great reader, and we had plenty of books. We were the only passengers, and ate our meals with the Captain and Officers.

This was the first of many transatlantic trips for me. Later ones were always with George, twice on the *Queen Mary*, once on the American *SS Independent*, once on a banana boat to the West Indies, and many times by plane. These crossings of the Atlantic in 1946 gave me a greater awareness of the size of the ocean than later journeys, in much greater comfort, would ever do.

CHAPTER XL

Travelling with the Family

The winter of 1947 was bitterly cold, and the snow lay until late March. The water-main froze outside the back-door, and in order to keep the central heating and hot-water boiler going buckets of water from a rainwater reservoir below the back garden had to be carried up two flights of stairs to the tank in the attic. Mr Woodcock worked valiantly at this; all the able-bodied members of the family helped. I did not count myself as one of these, for Giles was born on the 4 February. The main thawed for two days then, then froze for two more weeks, an experience not to be repeated until the hard winter of 1961.

When the thaw came, we began to look forward to a summer holiday in Switzerland, since currency regulations had also thawed, and for the first time in eight years we could take the family abroad. Just as I have written at some length about my first trip to America, I will describe this first holiday with the children in Europe, because it did include some remarkable signs of grace.

We decided to include Vera in the party, and leave Lucy aged 3, and Giles the baby, with George's parents, and a Swiss girl who would help to look after them. The Vauxhall was fully loaded, with three grown-ups, and Dan, Ellen and William, when we set off at 4am on the 14 August. After 45 minutes at Canterbury looking at the Cathedral, with no other visitors, we arrived at Dover in time for the midday boat to Boulogne. We had seen unrepaired war damage in Kent, but there was much more in France and the roads were in bad condition, only improving when we got further south. The night we spent in a hotel in Soissons helped us to realise that although our rations had been reduced in England, the French were worse off in some respects. There was bread and jam for breakfast, but butter and milk were absent. But we set off contentedly, enjoying the sunshine in our open car, until suddenly a French car came up at great speed on a side road. Assuming it would stop for us, George kept his speed up, (it was all of 40 mph) and only at the last minute managed by a great swerve to the left to avoid a collision. We had forgotten, or never known, the old French rule of *Priorité à droit*.

We stopped and gave thanks to God for a miraculous escape, and went on in a more subdued mood. We lunched at a wayside café, and on reaching Dijon at 3.30 decided to try and get to Switzerland that night, giving the children and Vera a first experience of hair-pin bends in the Jura. We crossed the frontier at Pontarlier and arrived at Vallorbe at 8 o'clock. The children had been complaining, and asking every five minutes when we would arrive, but all that is forgotten in the glorious memory of finding a town not only picturesque, but *en fête* with a brass band playing in the square. We found two hotels side by side, and divided our large party between them, but all ate together. After Vera had taken the children to their rooms, and the band had dispersed, we asked our host if the car would be all right parked in the square. He assured us that it would, saying 'Il y'à la Police de l'autre côté; et d'ailleurs il y a toujours le Bon Dieu.'

We set off in sunshine next morning. France, like England, had looked drab, but Switzerland was glorious Technicolor, with bright paint and carvings, and window-boxes on every house with geraniums, begonias and petunias. The Vauxhall had been filled up with petrol, oil and water, but even so the radiator boiled when we were crossing the Col Marchairaz on our way to the Lake of Geneva. From there we drove up to Charmey, then quite a small village with one hotel where we stayed, There was time for a first mountain walk after tea, and several avalanche tracks were visible. After bed-time the children were discovered playing Avalanches with their bulky feather duvets (though that word had not yet reached England).

The owners of the Hotel des Sapins was also the Chef, but he found time to teach us the local songs, and acted as guide taking George and me up the Moléson, the 2,000 metre mountain which dominated the view. That was only a walk, though a steep one.

His son took George up the Wandflüh. which entailed a 5 am start. Vera and Dan accompanied them as far as the Hut.

We had not booked any hotels for the rest of the holiday, so George and I went with the car to find a base on the Lake of Geneva. We had started early on a clear sunny morning, and on our way saw the snow-covered peak of Mont Blanc. When we reached Vevey we boarded a paddle-steamer which took us round the east-end of the Lake. We landed at the last village before the French frontier, St Gingolph, and liked it so well that we booked rooms for the family in the Hotel du Lac. After picking up the car again at Vevey, we took a different route back, and the diary records that we needed refills of water and oil to get the Vauxhall over the Col des Mosses. We had some happy and leisurely days at Charmey. There were mountain streams in which we could all bathe, and the children played with their boats. I sketched, and there were easy walks nearby, as well as the two strenuous ones recorded.

We decided that we should also reconnoitre the Lake of Lucerne and find another hotel for the family there. We set off with the car open, but the first rain of our holiday forced us to close it. We found the ideal hotel at Beckenried, a very small town, and drove back, skirting Lucerne, but visiting Berne and Fribourg among other places on the way, 200 miles in all. It was my first visit to Switzerland, apart from one ski-ing holiday, and we made the most of these exploratory days without the children. The next day we set off again with the family and drove down to St Gingolph. In front of the hotel there was a stony beach, off which we all bathed in the Lake of Geneva, then unpolluted.

Next day Vera had her first day off, taking the Lake steamer to Lausanne for the day. We lazed in the sun, which had now returned, swam three times, and had motor-boat rides, all the more exciting because the wind produced some waves on the Lake. The next day we celebrated Dan's ninth birthday, and again bathed three times. After that it was time for George and me to set off to find our next holiday hotel, the one at Beckenried being unable to have us until 1 September.

167

This time we intended to explore the Lötschental, a valley running up into the Bernese Oberland from the Rhone valley. We had read about it in the *Geographical Magazine*, and found the villages high up the valley as unspoilt as their description led us to hope. That day we only took the car up the rough road as far as Kippel, where we had lunch, but we walked on to Wiler, and booked rooms at the only hotel. There were no cars up there, but we were told we might bring ours, and so we did with the family on the evening of the next day. Before that we drove up the most frightening road we had been on, to Grimentz, on the other side of the Rhone Valley, where we stayed the night, had a short climb to see Monte Rosa in the distance, drove down the hair-raising road, then back to St Gingolph in time for a swim and lunch, and set off again with Vera and the children and the luggage. Going up the track to Wiler we were surrounded by goats and children, who gave us the impression that no car had been up there before. When we reached Wiler the goats went off to their byres under the houses of their owners, where the cows were already being milked.

Next day the children were surprised to find that instead of the pure white rolls we'd been offered elsewhere, a large coarse brown loaf was put on the table. But there was unlimited butter and runny cherry jam to go with it. We all went for a one and a half hour walk up the side of the valley, with many little torrents to be crossed by stepping stones. On our return we drank apple-juice for the first time, a drink as yet unknown in England.

The day after was Sunday, and one reward for going to Mass at Kippel was seeing all the women in their Lötschental costumes, including the smallest girls, black dresses with coloured shawls and gold lace bonnets. In the afternoon we walked three miles up to the next village to see a procession of soldiers in Napoleonic uniforms, complete with band and flags. George and I went on for another two hours up towards the glacier at the head of the valley, and had a beautiful walk back looking at the mountains bathed in evening light. George's comment, added to our diary later, 'The high point of our holiday'. It was not actually the highest point he had reached, for he had ascended a mountain of nearly 3,000 metres with two fellow guests the day before.

The next day we all had an eventful drive up to the Furka Pass. It was the worst ordeal the Vauxhall had yet endured, and not only did the water boil, but the oil as well, blowing off the oil-tank top. We followed all the other tourists and paid one franc each to go right inside the translucent bluish ice of the Rhone Glacier. An equally steep descent brought us down to Andermatt and Altdorf, where we crossed the Lake of Lucerne on a car-ferry, and found a warm welcome at the Gasthaus Rössli at Beckenried. It was so close to the Lake that the children spent the next morning fishing from the balcony, and caught six tiddlers, which they put into a garden pond.

We heard on the news that all tourist travel from England would be banned after the 1 October, owing to the shortage of foreign currency, and were very thankful that we were already having our foreign holiday.

Our week at Beckenried continued the mixture as before, walking, bathing in the lake, rowing, and some sightseeing by car and steamer. When George and I went up the Niederbauern, we were told we could use a private cable-car rigged up by a farmer to shorten his journey to the valley. It looked like a farm-cart, and for the price of 50 centimes each we were raised hundreds of feet, and swung over a deep valley. The cart going in the opposite direction was weighed down by water and emptied itself automatically at the bottom.

Our climb was rewarded by a view over the Lake of Lucerne, and its surrounding mountains. Our enthusiastic account of this expedition was to lead to the most special sign of Grace of the holiday.

The next day was our last, and we had arranged to drive to Zürich and visit George's relations. When Vera was asked what she would like to do, she said she would stay by the Lake and sunbathe. To my surprise, George very firmly said that she should spend the day going up the Niederbauer, and to my even greater surprise, Vera agreed.

We drove to Zürich in a leisurely way, as befitted a Sunday, pausing at a quiet spot to have a short service with the children. George's Uncle Ernst and Aunt Marianne and their daughter Hedeli gave us a warm welcome and a lavish lunch and the family were sufficiently overawed to behave well. We drove on to Baden, where George's widowed Aunt Anni and her brother, Uncle Hans, were equally kind over tea. We explained to the children that this was the town in which their beloved Walton Granny had grown up. When we got back to Beckenried in the dusk, we heard Vera's account of her day.

After she had left the farmer's Zeil-bahn, she saw a party of people going up the slope ahead. She hung back, but they waited for her, welcomed her in Swiss-German, and made it clear that they would like her to join them. This she did. When the children had gone to bed, she told us the sequel. One of the party was a young artist, Karl Glaus, and before the day was over, though neither knew more than a word or two of each other's language, they were sure that they would spend their lives together. And so they have.

I will skip the story of our homeward journey, via Neufchatel, Vézelay, Paris and Chantilly, among other places, except to say that we went on being wonderfully guided and blessed. The sequel to Vera and Karl's meeting was that they corresponded, with the help of George as translator. Vera took lessons in German, and Karl lessons in English. The next April, Karl came to stay with us; he did some paintings of Pindars and its surroundings, and sometimes helped dig the garden. By the time he left, in July, the wedding was fixed for the following spring, in Greys Church. George gave the bride away, and Ellen and Lucy were bridesmaids.

We all missed Vera, Lucy aged 5 most of all. By now she had two younger brothers. Hugh having been born in the autumn of 1948. On our next visit to Switzerland we took Lucy with us, and left her with Vera and Karl in Zürich while we had a walking holiday, to see the May flowers in the mountains. We saw them at their best when after walking across the Grosse Scheidegg in melting snow, we found the meadows brilliant in the setting sun, with Grindelwald below. We staggered happily into the first hotel we came to, the Gletschergarten.

In 1946 my mother had bought a house in Falmouth, going back to the part of England that her mother came from, and where her eldest sister lived. Rock Moor would be occupied by my brother Charles and his family, but they took a summer holiday in the U.S.A. every other year, and gladly lent the house to us and other family members while they were away. Now we had two beautiful places at opposite ends of England to visit. When the family was increased by the births of Mary in 1952 and Mark in 1953, some of the children would go by train on their own. This had the advantage that a cabin trunk could be sent off 'Luggage in Advance' and never failed to arrive in time.

Before the older ones wanted to go on holiday independently, we had other family holidays abroad. In 1956 we took seven children in one car to stay in a chalet in the Toggenburg. George and I had explored the area on one of his business trips the year before. Vera and Karl by then had two daughters, and brought them to stay for a few days. George's parents stayed in a hotel in Wildhaus, the nearest village, and came for picnics with us. I spent much of that holiday cooking, but the next year we went by train to the Zillertal, in Austria, and stayed in a small hotel, which was much more restful.

Two years later we hired a Camping Coach on the railway station at Morar. That was an easy journey, since we could go all the way by train from Reading. Mary and Mark were left behind this time, with one of the devoted helpers whom I shall mention in the next chapter.

Our last holiday with all the family was in Ireland, in 1959 at Rosbeg, on the Donegal coast. We drove to and fro in and out of Northern Ireland without anxiety, everything seemed peaceful. The house we rented was close to the beach and the sun shone every day for two weeks in September. The high point of the holiday in two senses, was the day when we all, including Mary aged 7 and Mark aged 6 managed to reach the top of Slieve League.

When we had scrambled down we feasted on mackerel, caught by some of the family the evening before, cooked over a bonfire. We returned to Rosbeg after two years and had other holidays in Ireland later on, but this first one has left the most vivid memories. The weather was never as good again!

CHAPTER XLI

Helpers

We could not have enjoyed our life at Pindars so much, or gone for so many holidays, if it had not been for all the different people who helped us.

After seven years Mr Woodcock retired; while we were wondering who we could find to replace him, Gerald Agnew's gardener gave us the answer. Sir Charles Hodson, later Lord Hodson, who lived further up the village, had decided he could no longer employ two gardeners, so one of them might be available. Mr & Mrs Brakespear came to see us, and we liked each other. They needed a house, and we were able to make available the little lodge with two tall chimneys that stood at the top of the drive. It had been occupied up till that time by the Heal family, and Mrs Heal had helped in the house. She wanted to give this up and get a council house, which was impossible unless they were homeless. At their request we evicted them, they were allocated a house in another village, and the Brakespears moved in, to be our prop and stay for 29 years. It was only when they felt unable to go on working that we began to realise that we could not stay at Pindars for ever. Mr Brakespear's name was George; partly for that reason, and partly so that the children would be respectful, we called them Mr & Mrs Brakespear for many years and not until the children were grown-up did they become George and Nan to us. George B had trained in Lord Nuffield's garden a few miles away, had then joined the Army, and lost an eye in the retreat to Dunkirk. However, he managed remarkably well with his other eye, and even drove a three-wheeler car. Nan had worked in the stately home at Nettlebed belonging to Peter and Ian Fleming's grandparents, and her high standards helped us to keep Pindars presentable in spite of the children skir-mishing all over it. That is to say, all over it except in George's study. That was forbidden territory, except by invitation.

With Mr Brakespear's skilled help, George was able to carry out plans for improving the garden. We had already removed a hen-run from outside the walled garden, and planted apple-trees there. Now herbaceous borders were added, which survived the occasional attacks of a football.

I was fortunate in never having both to cook and look after the children for any length of time. We always had someone living in the house to help, who was willing to do either. The best of them managed to do both while I went off on business trips or holidays with George. For five years we had a real old-fashioned cook, Mabel Russell, with a real old-fashioned shape. It was lucky that we had a big kitchen, or she wouldn't have been able to move past the round table where we had family meals, only using the dining-room in the evening and at weekends. Her home was in the next village, Highmoor, so we kept in touch for the rest of her life after she left to look after her aged parents.

Yvonne from Switzerland came for a year and was followed by Trüdi, who was a neighbour of Vera's, and she keeps in touch with us.

Vi Pengilley who lived with her parents in the village, came to us first just to help with ironing and mending (Oh! that mending, in the days when all socks were made of wool, without synthetic fibres. I always had a bag of mending, and whenever my mother came to stay she would settle down with it in the hall by the fire, or in the garden in summer). When Mr & Mrs Pengilley were both dead, and the tied cottage had to be given up, we asked Vi to come and live in. She did, and stayed until some houses for the elderly were built almost opposite her old home. Even then she came to help us until we moved house. She had cooked for a school before coming back to look after her parents, so was undaunted by our numbers, which could be considerable when the family brought their friends home, as well as our visitors to whom I will devote a special chapter.

Among our helpers I will include our dogs. Pica, the Border collie joined the household in 1966. As a puppy, she became a good watch-dog and also developed a talent for running with a somewhat deflated football and joined in the family games, as well as the walks for which Pindars was an ideal starting point, with foot-paths going off in every direction through the woods and fields, including the centuries-old 'Pack and Prime Lane' that ran along the bottom of the valley. After ten years Pica was reinforced by Natasha, Tassie for short, who came to us aged 4, but with a gentle nature in spite of previous bad experiences. Pica chased the rabbits on Parson's Hill, but I found Tassie once tenderly playing with the young ones.

When these two had completed their lives, another Border collie, Beck, came. She resembled Pica in looks, but had two owners and a spell in a dogs' home before coming to us. She became a good friend and reliable watch-dog.

CHAPTER XLII

Education

We soon had to decide which schools the children would go to. The boys when they left the village school went to daily preparatory schools in Reading until they were nine, but there was no such school on our side of Reading, and we thought the travelling would take too long once they had much homework. Fred Ogilvie recommended Packwood Haugh, near Shrewsbury, where his three sons had all done well. In those days parents were not expected to visit more than once a term and few did, unless living nearby. British Rail provided a train which passed through both Reading and Shrewsbury, and 'Luggage in advance' took care of the school trunks. Our sons all have mixed feelings about their years there, but it did prepare Dan, Giles and Mark effectively for Rugby, Bill for Mill Hill, and Hugh for Marlborough. They all went on to Trinity College, Cambridge.

Ellen, Lucy and Mary were able to go to the Abbey School in Reading, which was nearer than any boys' school. For most of the time George took them, and often others as well, as far as Reading station on his way to London. Car-pool arrangements took care of the return journey. After a while Ellen preferred a different route, cycling to Henley and going by 'bus from there with her friends. They all gained enough A-levels for University entrance, although Ellen studied languages at Fribourg in Switzerland, did a secretarial course, became a successful journalist and then decided to go to the London School of Economics, George's old college.

Lucy went to St Andrews after being a V.S.O. for a year in Kenya, and Mary to St Hilda's, Oxford.

At home, they all helped to educate each other informally. Singing together was important, especially singing rounds. This was a good antidote to boredom on long car journeys before the

Dan and William
1949

George 1940

Rosemary 1947

Four generations of Goyders
William 97, George 62,
Dan 32, Andrew 2

C.B.E. 1976

use of car radios or tape-recorders. Sometimes we would sing after meals, especially at weekends. Then we ate at the mahogany table in the dining room, a table which in spite of its antiquity was also used for table-tennis. On the walls, looking somewhat surprised at this activity, were some Bartolozzi prints of Holbein portraits, which we had bought after our move. They soon felt like old friends, especially the members of Thomas More's family, and we only parted with them when we began to collect water-colour drawings after the heaviest expenses of education were past.

All the family learnt at least one musical instrument at some time; many of them have kept up their music in later life. When a clarinet, purchased with orchestral intentions, led to a saxophone, and the formation of a jazz-band by Bill, there was a new use for the cellar, now vacated by the coke-boiler, which had been replaced by an oil-burning stove in an outhouse.

The Steinway grand was used for some piano-lessons and practice, but it was soon supplemented with a pianola-piano in the back-sitting room. This room had many uses, and was often the subject of discussion in the Family Council.

The Council was inspired by a book called *Cheaper by the Dozen* by Frank B. Gilbreth and Ernestine Gilbreth Carey, two members of a family of twelve children. The book gave a hilarious account of their family life in the United States, and was enjoyed by all the children who were old enough to read, when it entered our lives in 1953. The Gilbreths had a family council, and we copied them. George found it already established when he came back from a Transatlantic trip. The minute book records that I had been elected Chairman, and Dan, Secretary. George was Treasurer, as he controlled the Family Finances. I see from the minutes that some years later he was promoted to President.

Many of the discussions were about responsibility for keeping various rooms tidy. There were several demarcation disputes about play-areas, often concerning the day-nursery, which after 1960 was also the Television Room. In 1961 a resolution was passed about the sandpit, which was under a beautiful copper-beech tree. The wording was 'That the Mark and Giles Motor-racing Equipe, and the Mary and Hugh Peaceful Farm should each have 3 consecutive days, rain or fine'. When we were going through times of financial stringency, some sensible suggestions were made. Ellen pointed out that the Oxfordshire County Council (who were already paying the girls' school fees) would pay for her bus fares, and William (not Bill yet) suggested that better care should be taken of bicycles, and that the owners should oil them. During a later financial crisis, it was suggested that telephone calls should be shortened. When a gift of money from my mother to all the children was reported, they discussed what proportion should go to charity, and to which charities.

In 1965 an Extraordinary meeting of the Council was asked for by one of the family, who felt that other members of the family were bringing too many guests home without warning. It was agreed that where possible guests should be put down in advance in an Engagement Calendar with the exception of Lame Ducks, who could come without notice. Two months later a meeting is minuted as an 'Even more Extraordinary meeting'. This was summoned to consider the action of the President in removing the television set three days earlier. He explained that he considered it an anti-educational influence, and the family had shown a lack of discrimination in using it. The minutes continue 'A heated and intense debate followed, concentrating on the moral rather than the practical aspects.... To backbench cheers the Chairman proposed that the television be restored, but that all possible discrimination be exercised in its use; if it were not then no discrimination could be exercised.' This resolution was adopted without a vote.

The Council continued to meet until 1969 with one final meeting in 1972. Much time was spent in considering the building of a tennis-court; in the end the boys outvoted the girls, arguing that it would be much cheaper to go on paying to use courts at Peppard or Henley. Fortunately for Lucy, the acquisition of a pony did not have to be sanctioned by the Council. She was lent an elderly pony, by the Pullein-Thompson family, famed writers of pony books. Later on another writer, my cousin Mary Bosanquet, let us have a grey mare on long loan, so that Lucy could ride with her friend Janet Martin. The Martins had replaced the Lloyds at the Rectory. Janet, her two brothers, and the Oveys from down the valley formed with our family the core of a Fellowship which was centred on the Church, and met after 8 o'clock communion for breakfast in one of their homes.

The Family Council discussed holiday and Christmas plans. An important part of Christmas was the setting out of the Gauge O model railway. The lines usually went all round the big hall, surviving the rushing feet of excited children. The family always regarded them as 'Daddy's trains' but the Minutes record a decision that Bill should be responsible for the lay-out, and in later years Giles took over.

When the question of membership for members' husbands or wives was discussed, it was agreed that until the wedding they could attend as observers, but once married, would become full members. Dan's wife Jean, Bill's wife Belinda, and Ellen's husband Dominique were all co-opted in turn. Lucy's first husband Geoffrey returned to the United States with her after their wedding, and the Council had faded out before there were any further marriages.

CHAPTER XLIII

Guests & Grandparents

The Visitors' Book shows that we made full use of our extra bedrooms. Both the geographical and the age-range covered are wide. A page for 1953 picked at random includes in the addresses New York, Massachusetts, the Seychelles, South-West Africa, Scotland, St Gallen in Switzerland, Dublin, Montreal, and the French Jura. Many of these names connect with George's business interests, which covered parts of Europe as well as taking him across the Atlantic. Sadly, he had to be away in May 1955, when we had a family gathering to celebrate my mother's 80th birthday, with eight people staying, and many more for the day. Later large parties, with many people to stay, would celebrate our children's coming-out and coming-of-age parties, often with dancing in the hall. We had put down a large Ghiordez rug over the parquet floor, which was taken up on these occasions. When younger children danced, as they often did to the sound of George's accordion, they danced on the rug with bare feet, because Mr John, from whom we bought our rugs, said that would be good for it. This thought pleased my mother so much that she enlarged on it in one of her poems. She could write poetry as well as paint and was a frequent visitor from Falmouth, until her death at the age of 90.

The thought of painting brings me to all the visitors who came to us because of a shared interest in William Blake. Geoffrey and Margaret Keynes came many times, and we had several visits from American Blake lovers. But the most interesting visit was from Jacob Epstein, who brought his wife to spend a day with us in 1957 when he was preparing to make the portrait head of Blake that was put up the following year in the Poets' Corner of Westminster Abbey to mark the Bicentenary of his birth. Epstein looked at all our Blakes, and then hardly stopped talking between lunch and tea, giving his opinion of different artists, including Blake. Over the family tea-table, George mentioned the German-American humorous poetry of Charles Leland and quoted a particular favourite of his 'Hans Breitmann give a party'. At this Epstein became really excited, and said he hadn't heard that poem since he was a boy in Brooklyn.

George had been on the Committee making arrangements for the Bicentenary, so we were present for the unveiling of Epstein's very forceful head of Blake in Westminster Abbey. Ellen, Lucy and a friend were with us, and after the ceremony Epstein invited us back to tea at his studio, where we saw more of his works, some finished, some in progress.

About this period, George's parents paid us a good many visits. We were trying to persuade them to move nearer to us, now that his father was nearly 90 and his mother 82. They did not always hear the telephone, which made it hard to keep in touch. Agreeing that life would be easier without stairs, they came to look at houses near us, but George's mother bewailed the ugliness of English bungalows, having seen more attractive ones in their American days. We decided the only solution was to build them a house, as we had land to spare. The local planning committee gave us permission, and Sam Lloyd, a distant cousin (but now to become, with his wife Jane, very good friends), designed a house in which the grandparents could occupy the ground-floor. Upstairs they would have a guest-room and bathroom. Sam planned the rooms so that they would be similar to those in their old home, Cedar Cottage, but even so it was a great ordeal for them to move at that age. They may have settled into their new home more happily because there was an interim of a few weeks when their old house had been sold and the new 'Upper Pindars' was late in completion. During that time they stayed with us, and to get back to their quiet life, and their own possessions, even in a new setting, must have been a relief. George's mother enjoyed eight more years of life and his father ten, though 'enjoyed' is not the word for the last two years of his life. They were made toler-able for him by a real sign of grace. His wife had a very devoted nurse caring for her at home before she died, and she said to her 'Find someone to look after Will'. A few hours after the funeral the nurse was driving back from Reading in the rain, and gave a lift to a girl at a bus stop. The girl was Portuguese, and was working at the big house in Cane End where Dan and Ellen had been to school. She was very unhappy there, and longing to leave. She did leave, and came to look after George's father, until he died. She was engaged to an Italian lorry-driver, whom she married in our church some months later, Granddad giving away the bride. They lived in the upstairs flat, staying on after his death until they could buy a house of their own.

The Visitors' Book shows that George's brother Cecil came over from New York for his mother's funeral. He was now in charge of Radio-Communications for the United Nations. Claude and his wife Eleanor, who had emigrated to Canada after the war, were unable to come, but a nephew from Switzerland and a niece from Holland with their spouses came and stayed with us. It was early in December, and very cold. We have a photograph of our sons carrying the coffin from the house to the church, through the snow.

Whilst Upper Pindars was being built, and for some time afterwards, George and I hoped that it would also be our retirement home. But it now seemed obvious that none of our children would ever want to take over the big house from us, and we would not want to overlook other people occupying the house. So, sadly, it was sold.

CHAPTER XLIV

Out and About

George and I were able to do a great deal of travelling, often combining a holiday with some special object. Our trip to Yugoslavia in the summer of 1966 was a good example. In that year the Liberal committee on Industrial Affairs (see chapter XXVII) suggested that he should go to Yugoslavia to see if there was anything to be learnt from their system of Workers' Participation. We were lucky enough to be allocated a very pretty and intelligent interpreter, Vera Andrassy, who sat in on all our interviews in Zagreb. When we visited the local news-paper the manager made it clear that the workers' interest was the most important consideration. There was usually a commu-nist party representative at these meetings, as well as a workers' representative, and I noticed that it was the latter who took the initiative in ordering the coffee and slivovitz, the local brandy, which were served as elevenses. The only exception was when we had an interview with the (female) Director of the Institute of Social Management, who offered us blackcurrant juice.

When we had completed our inquiries, we flew to Dubrovnik, and stayed in a hotel on the coast nearby, and then in a hotel which had been a monastery on an island on a lake on the island of Mlini, and swam and sketched. We felt we had made a real friend in Vera Andrasssy, who later on visited us at Pindars.

In chapter XXVI George has described his first visit to India. I was able to go with him on two later visits, in 1978 and 1980. We flew to Delhi, where he was again attending a Conference. We were met there by Hugh who for the past two years had been working for UNICEF in Hyderabad. He and Catherine, his wife, had found a very good friend in Veradarajan, an enlightened industrialist. He took us under his wing, if that is the right description of arranging a flying tour for us that included Jaipur and other places in Rajasthan, and then invited us to stay in his home in Hyderabad. His wife, Malati, gave us a warm welcome, and showed us her pictures. We had heard from Hugh what a good painter she was. After his lecture at the nearby Administrative Staff College, George was asked at very short notice to give another lecture in Ahmadebad. He asked for a few quiet days in which to prepare, and we were sent by car, through Mysore, to Coonoor in the hills where we stayed in an otherwise empty hotel and were fed on Irish stew and rice pudding, a relief after so much curry. The trip to Ahmadabad was made worthwhile by a visit to Gandhi's ashram, a place of great peace.

Our last visit to India was in the autumn of 1980. We went first to Nagpur to stay with Hugh and Catherine, and their eighteen-months old daughter Jessica. Hugh was by now working for Oxfam. They travelled by train with us to Madras, and on by train for a holiday by the sea at Mahalibupuram. We returned to Bangalore, for the official object of our journey, a conference of industrialists, to which there were several other English delegates.

In the middle of the conference George developed a raging toothache, which a local dentist failed to cure. We telephoned our own dentist, and made an appointment for the day after our return. We were told to check-in at Bombay airport at one o'clock in the morning. At half-past seven we were still in the departure lounge, and so were some hundreds of other people, many with young children, not enough seats and nothing to eat or drink. It was getting very hot; the glass doors that led out onto the airfield were opened, but a soldier with a gun stood by to stop anyone going out.

Was it the toothache, or sheer desperation, that gave George the effrontery to say to the soldier 'Let all these people go out and sit on the steps'? When the soldier hesitated he told the only lie I have heard from his lips 'I am a member of the British Intelligence and I order you to let them out'.

It was several degrees cooler outside. People came out, and sat down, and the pressure was relieved. After another hour our flight was finally called, and we left India without any inquiries into George's credentials.

While we were at home in Oxfordshire, I gradually took on more outside responsibilities. We had two cars now; one was needed for the afternoon school run, and also to take me to meetings of Mothers' Unions and Young Wives Groups where I talked about such subjects as 'Children and Television'. In the earliest years it was 'Children and the Cinema'. I enjoyed the chance to visit villages in the furthest parts of Berkshire and Buckinghamshire, as well as our own county. I worked for the local Liberal Party, finishing as Constituency Chairman. I once stood as a candidate for the Oxfordshire County Council, without wanting to be elected. It seemed important that the Liberals should be seen as taking part in that particular Local Election, in that particular place. Mary and Mark (in their teens) gallantly helped me canvass, although their political views were not the same as mine.

For some years I was on the case committee of an Adoption Society, deciding which babies should go to the parents on the waiting list.

Interest in the history of Greys Court, led me to start research into the life of its most famous owner, Sir Francis Knollys, a cousin and courtier of Queen Elizabeth; I deciphered his letters to the Queen in the Public Record Office. The most interesting covered the time when he was in charge of Mary, Queen of Scots. I was also interested in finding out about his 16 children, whose effigies surrounded their parents' elaborate tomb in Greys Church.

The long typescript produced as a result of my researches seemed of no interest to anyone. I put it away, and would have forgotten it but for a providential meeting between George and the editor of Longman's 'Then and There' series, Marjorie Reeves. She encouraged me to use the material in a book suitable for twelve-year-olds, and it was published under the title *An Elizabethan Family*. Choosing the illustrations, which all had to be contemporary, led me to the Bodleian and the British Museum. I was later commissioned to do a similar book covering the fifteenth century. The Pastons in Norfolk and the Stonors in Oxfordshire are both families whose letters from this period give a detailed picture of their lives and to my great satisfaction I found some links between them, so that I could weave the material into a continuous story.

CHAPTER XLV

Moving On Again

During the 60's and 70's our sons and daughters were marrying and settling into homes of their own.

The time came when Mary said to us 'You are overhoused'. We had to admit that she was right. The problem was the garden, rather than the house. George Brakespear had continued to look after it until he was 65, and even then mowed the lawns and grew the vegetables. We did not need so much space for these now that the family were less at home, and shared the rest of the vegetable garden with young couples, who each had their own plot. This still left too much for us to do in the shrubberies and flower borders, and I felt that I could not leave home between June and October because of all the fruit that had to be picked and preserved.

When we were house-hunting we had a clear picture in our minds of the house we wanted. It would have rooms high enough to house the Georgian bookcases from George's study and a small garden, and would be in a village with shops and other amenities. We did not succeed in finding a house like this in the Chilterns or Thames Valley.

Two of our sons, Dan and Giles, were by now living in Suffolk. On one of our visits we saw a possible house, and almost bought it then and there. Prudence prevailed, for it was not in the right kind of village, but we began to realise the advantages of moving to East Anglia. It did not seem likely that any of the family would settle in the Henley area. On our way home we stopped to have coffee with friends who had just moved from Farnham in Surrey. Their house in Clare was Georgian and had been the doctor's house. A few weeks later, thanks to Providence and an exceptionally helpful house-agent, we were looking at a similar house in the nearby village of Long Melford. George was sure that this was the answer to our prayers.

At first I was uncertain, but I soon came to agree with him, as I learnt more about the amenities of Long Melford. The house fronted on the main street, with a steady stream of traffic going past, but the garden at the back was quiet. It was small, because the doctor who had sold the house had kept half the land and built a bungalow behind. The oldest part of the house had been owned by a weaver called John Smyth in the fifteenth century, and passed through many changes before the Georgian front with the high ceilinged rooms was added in the eighteenth century. We had plenty of time to consider our decision. The owners had shown the house before they had actually decided to sell. After some months of waiting we moved at last, on my birthday in July 1979, after many good-byes and a farewell party from the village that had been the setting of our lives for 34 years.

It did not take long for us to become involved in new activities. George was very soon asked to join the Executive Committee of the Suffolk Preservation Society, and became its Chairman for three years. This involved driving all over the county, as he had to attend meetings in all the different districts. I often went with him, and it was a very good way of getting to know a new area. We had only one car now, so I decided to limit myself to working for organisations in the village. After a short time I became Secretary of the Parochial Church Council, and later of the Historical and Archaeological Society.

George was still working for legislation to change the industrial system in this country, and wrote another book, *The Just Enterprise*, published by André Deutsch in 1987. The ideas put forward in it are radical and have influenced many people, but the Thatcher years did not provide a favourable climate for a new philosophy of industry.

Since coming to Suffolk, I too have produced another book, as editor rather than author. Among our many new friends, I found several people who had been at my old school, Hayes Court, in its earlier years. Their memories were so lively, that I decided to collect those of others as well. The school only lasted 20 years, and seemed to have sunk without a trace on the outbreak of war in 1937. The result of my efforts was privately printed under the title *Hayseed to Harvest* and launched at a party of all the survivors whom I and a small committee could discover, in 1985.

Two years later there were more parties. In November 1987 we gave thanks for 50 very happy years of marriage at a special service, followed by a lunch-party, accordion-playing by George, and dancing by some of our grandchildren. At that time there were 22 of them, and they were all there, and so were our sons and daughters, who had organised the celebration.

The next summer we celebrated George's 80th and my 70th birthdays, with two parties, one at Mansel Hall, and one at the Reform Club.

The grandchildren have grown in number as well as size since then, and we now have one great-grandson. A sorrow shared by us all was the sudden death of Mark and Conca's second son, Robin Benedict, in his cot when two months old.

A family tree at the end of this book lists our sons and daughters, their wives and husbands, and children.

The Appendices explained

The six appendices (with one additional commentary)
illustrates the author's part in revising the Canon law
of the Church of England, 1951-64.

APPENDIX I a

Is a verbatim report of the speech made to the Church Assembly
on 20 June 1951 which introduced synodical government as
an essential prerequisite for revising the Canons.

APPENDIX I b

Gives the reaction of the *Church of England Newspaper*.

APPENDIX II

The text of the author's speech on inter-communion (14 June 1955).
This speech was widely quoted, despite the opposition
of the Archbishop of Canterbury, who frequently ruled it
out of order.

APPENDIX III

Letter to the Archbishop of Canterbury (6 April 1954)
on the progress of the reform of Canon law.

APPENDIX IV

Letter to Lord Hailsham (4 March 1955) commenting on the
changing relations of Church and State and urging the formation
of a Parliamentary Group to monitor the revisions of Canon law.

APPENDIX V

Memorandum on Church/State relationships for consideration
by the Parliamentary Group (13 October 1955).

APPENDIX VI

A list of the speeches made in Church Assembly and National
Synod (1949-75) taken from the *Report of Proceedings*.

APPENDIX I a

Canon Law Revision

Mr G Goyder (*Oxford*) moved:

'That the Assembly welcomes the revision of Canon Law as a valuable contribution to the establishment of good order in the Church of England and commends the process of revising the Canons to the attention of the Laity of the Church.'

He said: I am conscious of the responsibility which falls to me in moving this motion on Canon Law. I hope I shall be given the grace to speak with accuracy, with clarity and with reasonable brevity. In order that I may not be accused of inaccuracy, I would wish the Assembly to study the Motion for a moment, and in particular the fifth word of it, which is the little word 'the'. The reason I say this is that I wish that word 'the' to be taken in the general sense rather than the particular sense. I wish that because I should be sorry if the Chairman were to rule me out of order if I referred in general to the revision of Canon Law as well as to the particular revision which is now being undertaken by the Convocations.

It will be generally agreed by this Assembly, I take it, that the Church, in Common with all human organizations, needs to have rules of conduct; and I take it that the first reason for the laity welcoming the new Canons that are being considered by the Convocations is the fact that the very consideration of the new Canons, after 348 years, is surely evidence that the Church is awake to the importance of affirming the reign of law and order. It is, I take it, an affirmation by the Church, after this long time, on the side of law and order in the Church and outside it.

That, I think, is a great thing. I have repeatedly in this Assembly referred to the importance of upholding the moral law from which the seventh Article of our religion tells us that no Christian man whatsoever is free.

We were told on Monday by Your Grace in the House of Laity that the laity have no constitutional position as of right in the making of Canons, and that being the case, I think that we – if I may speak for the House of Laity – would wish to thank the Convocations for graciously inviting the laity to consider the Canons and to pass up any observations that we may have.

I take it that we have all read the Canon Law Report; if we have not, then we ought to have done so. It will be noted that the basis taken for the revision of the Canon Law is that of the 1603 Canons, and I feel that at the outset it is necessary for us to consider together what gave rise to the 1603 Canons and what followed them.

The fact is that the 1603 Canons were the cause of the first serious spilt in the Church of England after the Reformation. They divided the clergy and the laity, with disastrous consequences to the Church of England.

According to Gwatkin, in his *Church and State to the Death of Queen Anne* (page 274), 'The Canons of 1603 were compiled in the narrow spirit of Bancroft, aimed especially at the Puritans, and scattering excommunications almost as recklessly as the Council of Trent.'

Professor Gooch, in his *English Democratic Ideas in Seventeenth Century*, says that the Canons of 1603 'were regarded by later generations as the fountain head of the doctrine of absolutism, and thus a few years after the death of Elizabeth the Nation was divided into two camps, the King and Church on one side – Parliament and Puritans on the other.'

Frere's comment is similar. He says that by the Canons and their after-math 'the Church entered on a false alliance with untenable royal claims to absolute government, while the Puritans allied themselves with Parliament'.

If I see a danger of the same thing happening today, it is not because I think that the authors of the Canon Law Report would wish such an event to take place; it is because the authors of the Report took as their basis a set of Canons which themselves arose out of an historic situation and brought about an historical situation both of which proved to be disastrous to the Church.

It needs to be remembered that the Canons of 1603 were never accepted by the laity. At that time there was no Church Assembly – unfortunately – but in Parliament, which represented the lay mind, the Canons were rejected; and so it is that we as laymen are not bound by the Canons of 1603.

I am sorry to say, but I must say this for the sake of accuracy, that I regard the present proposed revision as reflecting to some extent the narrow, the intolerant and the highly ecclesiastical spirit in which the 1603 Canons were compiled. (Several members 'No.') That is just my personal view.

In another connection recently, I suggested that responsibility to the consumer is a valid principle of industrial organizations, with which I have some little familiarity; and I would suggest that the same principle applies to the Church. When one examines the matter from the point of view of respon-sibility to the consumer, there are a few straws in the constitutional wind which help us to arrive at a judgement of the matter, although there are not many.

The difficulty in discussing the Canons is the fact that there are so few precedents. We have to go back more than one-sixth of the way to the birth of our Lord before we reach the 1603 Canons, whereas there are only seventy years intervening between the Reformation in this country and the passage of the 1603 Canons. If I go back a moment another seventy years, I hope the assembly will pardon me, because at the Reformation the clearest possible indication was given of the intention of the bishops, the clergy and the King at that time with regard to the making of the Canons.

In 1537 the first doctrinal book of the Church of England was published. It is a very important book, as Professor Dibden and more recently Davies in his *Episcopacy and the Royal Supremacy*, have ponted out. It is a book which, because it is very rare, has hardly received the attention that it deserves. I believe that there are only half a dozen copies in the world, but it has been reprinted once. It is known to historians. In that book it was pointed out by the bishops, all of whom signed the *Bishops Book* as did all the archdeacons, that there are three offices of the clergy: first, the power to excommunicate; second the power to ordain; and third, the power of making rules and Canons for the Church. The book says that the Canons are to be made 'by the ministers with the consent of the people, before such times as princes were christened and after they were christened with the authority and consent of the said princes and their people'.

Thus we have at the outset of the Reformation a declaration by all the bishops and all the senior clergy that in the making of Canons the laity are to have the right to assent. I was indeed very grateful to Your Grace when on Monday you told us that, as a matter of grace but not of right, it was proposed that at some later stage the steering committee of the laity would perhaps discuss matters with the steering committee of the Convocations. I do not know whether your Grace realized that you were reasserting an old principle, but in fact the four commissions which were appointed to look into the Canons when Henry VIII took the matter into his own hands were all of them commissions in which the laity were to have an equal share – sixteen members of the laity and sixteen members of the clergy. (I hope I may be forgiven for putting the laity first; it is my natural bias!) There was no mention on Monday that the laity were to have an equal right in the present revision of the Canon Law; nor does one find any mention of it in the Canon Law Report. I think it would have been most interesting if the authors of the Canon Law Report had mentioned the fact that there are these four historical precedents for the laity being joined to the clergy in the consideration of the Canons – and of course, as the Assembly knows, the 1571 Canons were produced by that joint committee.

I wish in a few minutes to suggest four principles on which I believe that the revision of the Canons, which I personally welcome, should proceed.

The first principle I suggest is that the Canons should be such as will edify the whole Church – the whole Laos or people of God. That means that the People of God, which includes the laity, should decide these matters together. This is not inconsistent with the fact that the office of bishops and clergy is quite dissimilar from that of the laity. It is, as I see it, for the bishops to initiate and define and for the laity to assent, but assent carries with it the right of dissent, and the right of assent and of dissent is a totally diverent matter from a mere right of looking at the thing. That is obviously a very important constitutional point.

The desire of men and women for a degree of self-determination is now universally recognized, in countries outside the Iron Curtain, in respect of politics. Why not in the Church, too? Archbishop Benson pointed out in his Life of Cyprian that the early Church set an example in democracy. He said that the First Council of Carthage was 'the only free, the first representative Assembly of the world'.

'The best system of Church polity and the one most expressive of the mind of Christ is that which gives fullest play to all the powers of the Body corporate and its individual members. The maxim that what concerns all should be approved by all is a principle of ancient law which has had great influence in English constitutional law. But it is more than a principle of law, we believe it to be inherent in the Gospel.' Why do I say 'we'? I say 'we' because I have not been using my own words, but quoting from the Joint Committee which reported to Convocation of Canterbury in 1902 on the 'Position of the Laity'. This Joint Committee consisted of seven bishops, including London, Salisbury, Wells, Bristol and Litchfield. The Report was received and formed the basis for the establishment of the National Council.

I will quote one or two other things which that Report said. It said: 'It seems entirely reasonable that the laity should be consulted and their approval obtained through their representatives before the enactment and promulgation of rules which concern them as the people of Christ.' That, of course, refers to the making of Canons.

There are two observations I should like to make. One is that the right of approval carries with it the right of disapproval. The other is that this passage is referring specifically to the making of Canons.

I should like to suggest to Your Grace that it might be helpful if that Report of 1902, which was a very substantial Report and was issued by the S.P.C.K., were to be reprinted so that the members of Convocations who will be considering these important matters may be able to refresh their memory on the rights of the laity in the Church.

The conclusions of the Report are: "We percieve very clearly both from the historical and theological portions of the New Testament, that the ultimate authority and right of collective action lie with the whole body, the Church".

Therefore, I take it to be the first principle of Canon Law revision that the laity should be accorded their scriptural and proper rights. which they have not been hitherto, by the Convocations in this particular revision.

I should like now to speak less controversially for a momnent and to refer to the fact that in the Anglican communions overseas this right about which I have been speaking has been granted. The churches of Canada, the United States, Australia and New Zealand have long since decided that in these days the laity should be brought in to all Church matters, not merely matters of business but matters of principle which concern them, including the making of Canons.

I recently returned from the United States, and there I went into this question with some of the clergy. I was told by a well-known American bishop that the clergy and the laity sit together in a single House as a matter of course, and the bishops sit separately and have the right of veto. There are two Houses, and that seems to me to be a very workable arrangement, with several advantages – one of which would be that when we passed a budget, as we did this morning, we should be able to save a good deal of money.

I believe that this corporate action of the Church should apply to this country. I believe that the time has come when the home Church should restore this position, and I believe that the revision of the Canons provides the opportunity. I commend this suggestion to the Convocations.

Has not the time really come now for us to put this matter right. If we are to ask the State to grant the Church more freedom in relation to its Liturgy – and of course, in the Canon Law there is the suggestion that the Convocations should be authorized to vary the liturgy in certain respects and that the diocesan bishops should do so, too, under the Lawful Authority Canon – if we are to have that authority, surely we must recognize that that right which has existed in the laity ever since the Reformation, if it is to be taken away with one hand by the removal of the authority of Parliament, even in part, must be compensated by the granting of the same right within the Church by the clergy. If I may say so, I think it is a little bit disingenuous of the Archbishop of York and others to think that Parliament will, on the one hand, give up the rights which ever since the Reformation it has jealously guarded on behalf of the laity, and, on the other hand allow the Church to place the laity in a position – as is now suggested by the Report – in which they have not found themselves since the Reformation.

To my mind, nothing gives greater offence in the Church than occasional disagreement between clergy and their parishoners about the order of service. This may apply to only a few of the clergy, but it is a fact that when ceremony is imposed on a congregation, it causes offence, particularly in country parishes. Not long ago I was told a story of two churchwardens who remonstrated with a new vicar for imposing a ceremonial which the parishioners did not like and for having emptied the church; and the vicar's reply was. 'I do not really mind; I see an angel in every empty seat.' The answer of the churchwardens was, 'Yes, but they don't put anything in the collection.'

In a few days' time you will be receiving, or will be able to buy, a report by the Church Information Board on the 'Financial Resources of the Church'.

This report will be of immense importance, because it will show that in ten years the Church has lost half of its revenue through the fall in the value of money. Surely this must mean that the Church must expand. Evangelism is no longer an optional subject but a compulsory subject for the Church. I suggest that the bringing of the laity into the full government of the Church is a valid principle of Canon Law reform as well as a practical principle for today.

This brings me to my second principle; it is that nothing in the Canons should bind unnecessary burdens on the laity.

Once again, I want to refer to the *Bishops Book*, which is of great importance in this matter. It says that so far as concerns outward ceremonies and such things as are of themselves mean and indifferent – 'that is to say neither commanded expressly in Scripture nor necessarily contained or implied therin' – strict obedience is not to be required to any rules of the Church 'but men may lawfully omit or do otherwise than is prescribed by the said laws and commandments of the priests and bishops so that they do it not in contempt or despite of the said power and jurisdiction, but have some good and reasonable cause so to do – For in these points Christian men must study to preserve that Christian liberty wherunto they be called and brought by Christ's blood and His doctrine. This rule and Canon men must diligently learn.'

Thus the *Bishops Book* laid down at the outset of the Reformation that there should be a Canon of Charity. There is no Canon of Charity in the suggested Canon Law revision. On the contrary, Canon IX would make the laity liable to be delated, as the Scots like to say, by their parish priests for any failure to attend on one of the Saints' days or any failure to bow at the name of our Lord, or any other failure, and they would lose office in the Church if they were to fail in any of these things. They could be hauled before an ecclesiastical tribunal. I suggest that if the laity are to be put into this posiion, they should at least have the Canon of Charity, which the bishops in 1537 suggested should be incorporated in the Canon Law of this country.

My third principle is that the passing of new Canons must mean that the clergy accept law abidingness as a principle. There are many laws with which I personally do not agree that His Majesty's Government pass, but that does not free me from the obligation to obey the laws. The same cannot entirely be said of some of the clergy. I wish to comment on that only by reading a passage from that great Anglican Church man Jeremy Taylor, who said: 'Nothing is more usual than to pretend conscience to all the actions of men which are public and whose nature cannot be concealed. The disobedient refuse to submit to laws and they in many cases pretend conscience. Every man's way seems right in his own eyes, and what they think is not against conscience, they think or pretend to think is an effect of conscience, and so their fond persuasions and fancies are made sacred, and conscience is pretended, and themselves and every man else is abused.'

I take it to be the case that the fact that we are to have new Canons, which we welcome, is in itself a declaration by the clergy that in future the spirit of law abidingness shall govern the actions of the Church. There is a distinction between variations of detail in the liturgy in the spirit of charity and in the spirit of law abidingness and the deliberate disobedience to the law of the land which, I suggest, puts the Church in a great difficulty in the eyes of the laity, because some of us feel that almost the first duty of the Church is to express that spirit of law abidingness which is incumbent upon them.

My fourth principle is that nothing in the Canons should militate against re-union. Here I want to refer for a moment to Canon XI which, if passed by the Convocations in its present form, would shut the door on all re-union for our time, because it would crystallize and harden a situation which is surely only temporary. I think that this Canon should be looked at with the greatest of care by the Convocations. I take it to be a principle with which the Assembly would agree, I hope unanimously, that the whole question of re-union should be kept in mind and that no Canon should be passed which in itself would slam the door on any of the proposals for re-union which are so much in people's minds today.

I have mentioned four principles, and I repeat them. First, the right of the laity to full participation in the government of the Church as practised overseas in the Anglican Communions and as recommended in the Report of the Convocations in 1902. Secondly, that no unnecessary burdens should be imposed on the laity but that in all these things not expressly commanded in Scripture the Canon on Charity should govern. Thirdly, that there shall be a determination from now on to abide by the law on the part of all of us. Fourthly, that none of the new Canons should impede or make more difficult the process of re-union.

I apologize for speaking at some length, but this is an important matter. I hope that this debate will have the result of establishing principles for a godly order uniting Christians in the National Church and that the laity will play their part; and that all of us, by this debate today, will be united rather than divided in a determination to be what we are intended to be, the Laos of God.

The Church Assembly

Last week the Church Assembly fully justified the claim, sometimes made on its behalf, to be the finest debating assembly in the country. Not unnaturally, there is a lack of that procedural polish which only a legislative body in continuous session can achieve. Professionalism is replaced by a spontaneous *ésprit de corps* and a respect for the still yet young tradition of ecclesiastical democracy. To all this the geniality combined with firmness and the frequent concessions to informality of the Chairman, the Archbishop of Canterbury, make a large contribution. Theoretically, advantage might accrue from having a neutral chairman. The Archbishop is intimately associated with the policies under debate. It is rather as if the Prime Minister or Leader of the Opposition were to preside over the House of Commons. But there is no sign that any cause which the Archbishop has espoused obtains preferential treatment or that his critics receive the disadvantage of the doubt.

In the Assembly the Church of England has an institution of which to be proud. That typically British tendency to self-depreciation which so often leads to an attitude of tolerance and humility has also led to wholly unreasonable criticism. If Church of England people talk at all about the Assembly they do so apologetically. For that there is no need whatever. Boasting would be more appropriate. Had the Communists any such remarkable institution the whole world would know about it, but they have never been capable of producing one, and have therefore been obliged to fall back on the primitive methods of despotism. Out of the maturity of British democracy coupled with the mutual respect which is the fine flower of the Christian faith has emerged an institution whose potentialities, even after thirty years, are not half realised.

Debate proceeds with good tempered restraint, with high dignity, and yet with refreshing and vigorous wit. Dull periods are inevitable but even these become instructive as the result of a healthy tendency to reduce details of administration to first principles. Only minds with a strong mastery of their subject can do this but again and again what could run out into the deserts of superficiality is made responsive to the demands of realism. Essentials do not look for concealment in forests of verbiage or technicality. It is not that one or two oratorical giants dominate discussion. That is far from being true. If there is little of excelling brilliance, the average level of the speeches, both clerical and lay, is higher than the level of mere competence. Where genius would mean risk, great ability is virtue. Large theories, such as the theological status of Freemasonry, receive treatment that is worthy of them.

Obviously, such an assembly would bear with ease the heaviest weight the Church could place upon it. *That was the purport of Mr George Goyder's outstanding speech on the function of the laity in Canon Law revision* [Author's italics]. Church Assembly could with advantage to everybody take over from Convocations the full burden of this work. That would ensure that the voice of the rank and file in the congregations was adequately represented. *Mr Goyder had put into the preparation of his speech a volume of research which challenged the claim of the House of Clergy to a monopoly of expert knowledge.* There were precedents for the association of the laity in the legislation of Canons and he was able to quote them. But that is only the beginning of the question. The whole purpose of a democratic, representative assembly is precisely that it is not a committee of professional specialists. It brings to bear on the problems of government the common sense of the intelligent citizen who sees the subject as a whole, instead of in parts. Besides that, whereas a hierarchical society tolerated and admired a hierarchical Church, a more egalitarian society will require a different arrangement. This also, incidentally, is an argument for introducing a stronger proletarian element into the Assembly: Church Assembly having won its spurs, Convocations might well withdraw into voluntary and permanent retirement. Their cumbrous machinery is obsolete. Their rattling pistons should give place to a jet engine.

It is highly improbable that Mr Goyder really believes this revolutionary change will occur within so short a time that Canon Law revision could reasonably suffer postponement until afterwards. He would be optimistic indeed if he hoped the Church would move as quickly as that. With all respect, the Church of England is not supersonic! In fact Mr Goyder may, in this case, have applied a valid general principle to an inappropriate particular instance. If the House of Laity are squeezed out of Canon Law revision the fault will be their own. Psychologically, morally, and especially politically, it would be quite impossible for Convocations to override the Laity either as regards the Law as a whole or as regards individual canons, if their hostility were clearly and firmly expressed. Unless the Church's leaders are possessed of a folly beyond characterisation they will not repeat the mistakes of 1927 and 1928. They will not ignore a strong body of representative opinion, even a minority.

What Mr Goyder has achieved, and the debate subsequent to his speech proved that he is not without powerful support among bishops and clergy as well as among his unordained colleagues, *was to assert the principle of lay responsibility*. He has clearly given notice that the Laity will play their part, and that this will be no insignificant part. They will not accept a role as extras or noises-off. This may turn out to have been an historic occasion.

The Church of England has the potentiality of creating within itself a system of government, founded on definite theological presuppositions, which will have much to teach secular politics. Within the Church at the present time are the materials for reconciling the age-old contradictions between liberty and order, individualism and collectivism, democracy and authority. Where the State has lost its sense of direction the Church can once more lead the way. That is a task worthy of the ablest ecclesiastical statesmanship.

Church of England Newspaper

Reunion: The Next Step

Speech delivered at the Church Assembly on 14 June, 1955 by George Goyder (Delegate of the Church of England to the second Assembly of the World Council of Churches at Evanston.)

At Evanston we felt with the force of a high wind the impact of the worldwide drive towards Christian unity. It was driven into us by the young Churches of Asia who spoke of the difficulty of mediating the Gospel through a divided church. It was impressed upon us by the main theme, and by Dr Schlink who said in his opening address:

'if we really hoped for Christ's appearance then we should have less fear of men and more of God...Then we should see clearly the provisional nature of our ecclesiastical activity, of our dogmatic formulations. We would not be so much in love with our own confessions, our own denominations, but would see Christ at work all over the world.'

Most of all we felt it in private conversations with laymen from other Churches. The question I was most frequently asked at Evanston is: 'What is the matter with the Church of England? Why are you dragging your feet in the movement towards unity and why are you so divided?'

I wonder if we are as divided as we seem? One serious difficulty is uncertainty about the position of individuals in other churches who wish to come to our Communion. It is clear that it is no part of the Anglican heritage to debar members of other churches from communion with us. The late Bishop of Oxford speaking in the Upper House of Convocation on the 27 May 1948 (on the Communion canon and Confirmation rubric) said:

'it is well known and indisputable that occasional conformity of persons not confirmed and indeed not belonging to the Church of England was allowed, and sometimes even encouraged, in the 17th and 18th centuries.'

I will not dwell on the 18th century for obvious reasons, but the 17th century was a spiritual peak. A former Dixie Professor of Ecclesiastical history in the University of Cambridge has written that there is no evidence in the 17th century that nonconformists were ever refused Communion with us because they were not Confirmed. The present Dixie Professor has martialled the evidence to prove that intercommunion was the general practice of our Church in the first two centuries after the Reformation.

Perhaps someone may think these historians suspect, as Cambridge men. Turning to Oxford we find Bishop Stubbs who was described by Gladstone as 'the first historical authority of the day' (and his day came after the tractarians) held the view that the Confirmation rubric does not apply to members of other Churches who wish to come to our Communion. Of Presbyterians he says:

'I do not think the Presbyterian was in the eyes of the Church when the rubric was inserted.'
And he adds:

'I think it more dangerous to repel a person from the means of grace than to risk something on his or her personal qualifications!'

The other great Church historian of the late 19th century was Mandell Creighton, Bishop of London. (It is true that he moved from Oxford to Cambridge in later life but he was sound in his youth.) Creighton says that when members of other Churches attend our Communion they are to be regarded as fit for confirmation in spiritual knowledge and may therefore be admitted to communion. With Stubbs and the Cambridge historians Creighton rejects the view that the Confirmation rubric is intended to apply to non-anglicans.

But the evidence is plainer than history, for it lies open in the pages of our Book of Common Prayer. In the eighth rubric to the Communion Service we find that every *parishioner* is required to come to Communion three times a year. And in all our Prayer Books prior to 1662 every person, whatever his church affiliation, is required to take Holy Communion at the time of his or her marriage. The Confirmation rubric could not possibly apply in these cases. In the controversy over the Test Acts and Occasional Conformity Bills at the end of the 17th century, no one disputed the right of members of other churches to come to our Communion although not confirmed.

The constitutional position also seems clear. Speaking in the House of Lords in June 1920 the Lord Chancellor told the Archbishop of Canterbury:

'unless a person is an open and notorious evil liver or a depraver of the Book of Common Prayer, as the law stands today he is entitled to have access to Holy Communion'.

I know the subject is delicate but I would venture to remind the House, in the words of the present Bishop of Exeter, that even when the Royal Licence and Assent are obtained for the new Canons, they will still be void and without effect if they are found to offend against the Statute Law or against any custom of the Realm.

I believe that the custom of admitting members of other Churches to our Communion is so historically continuous and widely established, that it cannot be affected by the Canons, even if it were not protected, as I believe it is, by the Statute Law of the realm and written into the Prayer Book. This however means that the resolutions made by Convocation in 1933 and any regulations the Bishops may have made under them since are without authority. The Convocations appear to be on dubious foundations in this matter; personally I should say they are ineffective resolutions and if so this ought to be generally known.

But there is an even simpler criterion. As a Catholic layman I ask myself 'What Catholic principle has been compromised by the admission of nonconformists to our Communion?' And I would ask the House to note that if such a principle were to exist, our catholicity would have been compromised for the past three centuries. But we find on the contrary that our greatest defenders of episcopacy also support intercommunion. Among the great men of our Church who defended episcopacy as of Divine institution in the 17th century were Lancelot Andrewes, Joseph Hall and Jeremy Taylor, and the first two were bishops.

All three wrote in defence of episcopacy. And all three wrote welcoming non-episcopalians at our altars. Let Jeremy Taylor stand for all such defenders of our episcopal order. He says that to make the way to Heaven narrower than God made it or to deny to communicate with those whom God will vouchsafe to be united and to refuse our charity to those who have the same faith because they have not all our opinions and believe not everything necessary which we overvalue, is impious and schismatical.

So in the eyes of these great Catholic Christians it is we who are the schismatics, when we deny the right of other Christians to join with us in Holy Communion. I want to ask the House:

'Why do we put up barriers our forefathers in the Church did not erect? Are we being honest about Re-union? Or are we running away from it under a barrage of words?'

I have mentioned the historians. The practice of our Archbishops in the late 19th century followed them. Archbishop Tait maintained throughout his primacy the right of nonconformists and presbyterians to come to our Table. He threw the responsibility for attending on the individual conscience of those who wish to join us. He did not forbid them. Presbyterians he welcomed, and so did Archbishop Benson who succeeded him.

I maintain we should do the same and I am talking only of individuals who desire to join us as an occasional act of hospitality or to express their solidarity with us.

We are about to embark on discussion with the Church of Scotland. To stiffen the terms when we are sitting down to negotiate is not the way to seek a settlement. It is not the way to treat an honourable and historic established and national Church to which the loyal subjects of the Queen in Scotland are attached. For centuries Presbyterians have been welcome at our Communion as we to theirs. They should be made officially welcome now in accordance with the ancient custom of the Church of England as we find it in the Book of Common Prayer.

But there is higher ground than history, or custom, or the Prayer Book, or the constitution, for maintaining the right of non-conformists and presbyterians to come to our altars and indeed of welcoming them as individuals, and that is the ground of charity as it is found in Scripture. They are our brothers in Christ. We invite them because it is Christ Himself who has invited us to join as brothers at his table. With Hooker we account all those members of Christ's Church who call upon the name of Our Lord Jesus Christ. It is an error to define the Church not by what the Church essentially is, but by what we imagine is more perfect in ours than theirs.

We have a custom in the Church of England of receiving members of other Churches to Communion with us. I believe today this custom needs to be reaffirmed. It is for our Bishops to make it plain that the members of other Churches are welcome at our Communion.

Full Reunion may be our aim, but it cannot be right to close the door on intercommunion while we discuss it. Real reunion will come about only as the Holy Spirit is given freedom to work His Will amongst us. It is the Spirit and not we, who brings about reunion.

Letter to the Archbishop of Canterbury

6 April 1954

My dear Lord Archbishop,

Thank you for your letter of March 31st. I am glad to know that the position of the Canon regulating the admission of members of other Churches to Communion is fluid enough to be reviewed and revised so as to provide for the historic position regarding hospitality and occasional conformity. I hope this can be done before the canon goes to the House of Laity.

As regards the Marriage Canons, it is my earnest hope that they too will be reviewed and revised before going to the House of Laity so that nothing in them further divides us from the Free Churches, or endangers the State connection, or our own unity. In particular a sure channel for re-admitting divorced persons to Communion is needed. I cannot think that the present method of episcopal regulation can remain if the clergy's legal right of discretion is to be removed. Something more certain and more definite is needed.

These two groups of Canons, together with the position of the laity, are the only crucial issues I see in the whole proposed body of new Canon Law, with the possible exception of the Ecclesiastical Courts. I believe the difficulties in regard to the two latter are in process of solution and if the two former problems can be surmounted, the Canons would seem to be assured of general support.

My letter of 12 March had considerably more behind it than the Steering Committee meeting and reading it again in the light of this correspondence, I find that despite faults it says truly, and I believe accurately, what it was intended to say. I am sure your Grace will take account that my aim in writing was to avert a crisis, not to cause one. For this purpose it is better to be a year early than a day late. I appreciate the kindness and courtesy of your Grace's reply.

Yours sincerely,

The Most Reverend His Grace The Lord Archbishop of Canterbury,
Lambeth Palace,
S.E.1.

Letter to the Rt Hon. the Lord Hailsham Q.C.

4 March 1955

Dear Lord Hailsham,

As you know, the Church of England is in process of revising its Canon Law. Some of us who sit in the House of Laity of the Church Assembly are much concerned to see that in the process the Church does not become over-clericalised and on the positive side to see that the establishment is not undermined. Some of the more difficult problems we face are the Canons on divorce and re-marriage, admission to Communion, and the Ecclesiastical Courts. I am particularly concerned with the place of the laity and as a result of a speech I made two years ago in the Assembly, a Commission has been set up to see how the laity can best be joined with the clergy in the government of the Church.

Now that the Canons are being formulated it seems desirable to some of us that we should meet with interested members of the two Houses of Parliament to see if we can reach a common mind.

About fifteen of us who sit in the House of Laity and take a prominent part in the debates have been meeting privately during the Assembly sessions. Our next meeting will be on Tuesday, 14 June, at 6.30 for 7 pm, dinner and we shall meet at P.E.P.

We have decided to invite a number of Members of Parliament to join us. Lancelot Joynson-Hicks is already a member of our group and Eric Fletcher has agreed to come to this next meeting. I would be very glad if you would join us and perhaps you would suggest one or two other members of the House of Lords who would be interested. It is, of course, a private group and our proceedings will be confidential, for the time being at any rate. I thought of asking Richard Wood and Ralph Assheton and would like your advice on this.

At our meeting on 14 June we are going to try and clarify our view as to what should be the relation of Church and State under present conditions and what is the positive contribution of the State to the Church.

Without perhaps realising it you have already had some influence on the situation. It was largely as a result of your letter in *The Times* on the re-marriage of divorced people that I wrote to the Archbishop of Canterbury last February intimating that a group of us in the Church Assembly would not accept the proposed Canon and would, if necessary, bring the issue to Parliament. As a result of this I am glad to say the Archbishop has modified his policy but not, I fear, his convictions. I say this to you privately so you will understand that we are not just talking in the air but are dealing with matters of constitutional importance which are bound to become also of political importance in the not very distant future.

The Changing Relations of Church & State

The compact of Church and State is a political principle embedded in English history. Edward the Confessor thus declared the doctrine of the royal supremacy:

'The King, who is the vicar of the highest King is ordained to this end, that he shall govern and rule the earthly kingdom and people of the Lord, and above all things the Holy Church and that he defend the same from wrong-doers.'

Nearly half a millennium later, Stephen Gardiner, the leader of the High Church party at the Reformation, wrote:

'no new thing was introduced when the King (Henry VIII) was declared to be the Supreme Head: only the Bishops, nobles and people of England determined that a power which of divine right belongs to their prince, should be more clearly asserted.'

At the Coronation the nation saw the alliance of Church and State in dramatic form and realised again its deep significance. But the terms of the alliance are changing. In spiritual matters the Sovereign now represents her People constitutionally, through the advice tendered by her ministers, rather than personally. She is not, as the first Queen Elizabeth was, the one representative layman, but a constitutional Sovereign and Head of the Church in her representative capacity. This emphasises the importance of the advice tendered by her ministers in matters affecting the Church. At a time when relations between Church and State, never secure, are once more changing, it is desirable that Parliament and ministers of the Crown should be aware of the responsibility that will shortly fall upon them to advise the Sovereign in connection with the current revision of the Canons. These Canons contain some disturbing features.

The relations of Church and State are involved in the marriage Canons. The draft Canons propose to remove from the clergy their right under the Matrimonial Causes Act of 1857 to use their discretion in remarrying divorced persons in Church. There is ground for hoping that the Convocations will have second thoughts. As they stand the Canons would take away the right of the layman to a remedy provided for by an Act of Parliament, and similarly deprive the clergyman of his liberty provided by that Act.

Perhaps the most important aspect of the changing relations of Church and State is the position of the laity in the Church. Historically Parliament has represented the laity since the Reformation. But in practice Parliament acts today as a trustee rather than as a spokesman of lay rights in the Church. The draft Canons provide that the Convocations alone shall have the right to govern the Church. No place is given to the laity in determining doctrinal questions or in making Canons. This is a change from the Elizabethan Church Settlement. As Professor Neale has shown, the Prayer Book which, with slight changes in 1662, governs the Church's worship today was the work of the Parliament of 1559.

If the Church is to govern itself by Canons, the rights of the laity in the process of canon making become of increasing importance. The draft Canons provide no place for the laity in the process. This appears to be contrary to the intention of the Act of Submission, when a Joint Commission of clergy and laity was appointed by the Crown to supervise the making of Canons and to advise the Sovereign. There is a weighty body of opinion among Church historians that Canons to be valid require the assent of the laity. It should be remembered that while the present Canons have been held not to bind the laity, it is intended that the new Canons will be binding on the laity and make them liable to ecclesiastical discipline.

The laity's right of access to Holy Communion is affected by the canons. Church people have at present a right of access to Holy Communion, even though they are not Anglicans. Although attempts have been made to deny this right, it is known to be a well established and continuous custom and the rubrics to the Book of Common Prayer recognise it. The new draft Canons would remove this right from the laity and deprive the clergy of the discretion they now have to admit members of other Churches to Communion on occasion.

There is the question of the Church Courts. The Ecclesiastical Courts Commission recommends the elimination of the appeal to the Privy Council in ecclesiastical causes. It proposes to create a new clericalised Court with no appeal from it. This may affect the constitutional principle that there can be only one system of law in England and that it is the right of the Judges of the common law to determine it. The Report also proposes that the bishops shall have the right of veto in cases involving clerical discipline and breach of common law. This seems to revive the principle of 'benefit of clergy' discontinued at the Reformation.

These matters need to be viewed in perspective. The Church of England is in serious financial difficulty, postponed only by the recent successful financial operations of the Church Commissioners and the shortage of clergy. Both inside and outside the Church of England there is dissatisfaction with its party divisions and the lawlessness of a section of its clergy and this is the main reason for new Canons. The danger is that in the process of tidying up the law, the Church will cease to represent the nation and become a clericalised society at a time when a deep spiritual hunger is showing itself in the nation, as the success of recent evangelistic efforts testify, and at a time when the spirit of reunion is growing.

Parliament still represents the nation and the laity in the nation. The question Parliament will have to decide is the extent to which it wishes to delegate its rights to govern the Church to the laity in the Church and what residual rights it desires to maintain for the sake of the nation as a whole. All the Canons will require royal approval and some will require Acts of Parliament.

Our group of laymen in the Church Assembly came together because we felt the growing danger of a clericalised Church. It has been a holding action. The time has come for the question of the relations of Church and State to be put on a more positive basis. Can we, by taking stock of the position, agree upon the terms of a new and constructive alliance between Church and State, in keeping with the needs of the day? Parliament, through its historic right to advise the nation, has the power to protect the Church from taking a wrong course. It also has the power to assist in the re-establishment of a Church representative both of the clergy and the laity and more national in character than it can be said to be today.

13 October 1955

Speeches in the Church Assembly 1949-70 and in the National Synod 1970-75

Index

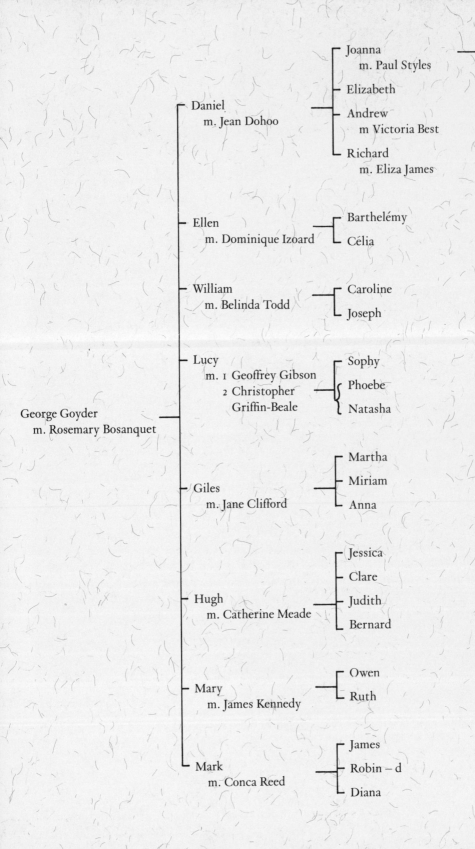

George Goyder
m. Rosemary Bosanquet

Daniel
m. Jean Dohoo

- Joanna
    m. Paul Styles — Felix
- Elizabeth
- Andrew
    m Victoria Best
- Richard
    m. Eliza James

Ellen
m. Dominique Izoard

- Barthelémy
- Célia

William
m. Belinda Todd

- Caroline
- Joseph

Lucy
m. 1 Geoffrey Gibson
2 Christopher
Griffin-Beale

- Sophy
- Phoebe
- Natasha

Giles
m. Jane Clifford

- Martha
- Miriam
- Anna

Hugh
m. Catherine Meade

- Jessica
- Clare
- Judith
- Bernard

Mary
m. James Kennedy

- Owen
- Ruth

Mark
m. Conca Reed

- James
- Robin – d
- Diana